MANNERS FOR KIDS

Essential Life Skills To Teach Our Kids

CORA WILSON

© Copyright 2023 - **All rights reserved.**

The content contained within this book may not be reproduced, duplicated or transmitted without direct written permission from the author or the publisher.

Under no circumstances will any blame or legal responsibility be held against the publisher, or author, for any damages, reparation, or monetary loss due to the information contained within this book, either directly or indirectly.

Legal Notice:

This book is copyright protected. It is only for personal use. You cannot amend, distribute, sell, use, quote or paraphrase any part, or the content within this book, without the consent of the author or publisher.

Disclaimer Notice:

Please note the information contained within this document is for educational and entertainment purposes only. All effort has been executed to present accurate, up to date, reliable, complete information. No warranties of any kind are declared or implied. Readers acknowledge that the author is not engaged in the rendering of legal, financial, medical or professional advice. The content within this book has been derived from various sources. Please consult a licensed professional before attempting any techniques outlined in this book.

By reading this document, the reader agrees that under no circumstances is the author responsible for any losses, direct or indirect, that are incurred as a result of the use of the information contained within this document, including, but not limited to, errors, omissions, or inaccuracies.

ISBN: 9781916768024

Contents

Introduction	v
1. BEING HUMAN	1
Ages and Stages	2
How to Teach (and Learn) Self-Awareness	7
Teaching Children About Boundaries	9
2. TEACHING MANNERS	13
Staying Calm	19
Be Clear, Heard, and Understood	20
Watch Your Words	22
3. BASIC MANNERS	25
Pleases and Thank Yous	26
Friendliness	27
Apologizing	27
Gossiping	28
Sharing and Taking Turns	29
Being on Time	30
Pets	31
Conversations	33
Dress for Success	34
Greeting and Departing	35
Introductions	36
Out and About	36
Doors	38
Invitations	39
Family Events	40
Playdates and Parties	41
Table Manners	42
Noise Levels	45
Basic Hygiene	46
Tidying Up	48

Shopping	49
Using the Phone	50
Emails and Messages	52
Social Media	53
Respecting Your Elders and Authority Figures	54
Respecting Diversity	55
4. RAISING A RESPONSIBLE KID	59
Building Responsible Minds	60
Household Chores	65
Age-Appropriate Chores	66
5. MANNERS CHALLENGES	69
Helping Children Improve Manners	69
Coming Late to the Manners Game	73
How Not to Raise a Liar	74
Bullies	78
6. SOME ESSENTIAL LIFE SKILLS FOR KIDS	85
Good Money Habits	86
Understanding Time	88
Finding Your Way Around	92
7. TEACHING KIDS SELF-CARE	95
What Your Body Needs	96
What Your Mind Needs	99
Conclusion	103
Bibliography	109
About the Author	111

Introduction

Thump! Thump! Thump!

Sitting across from me is Charlotte, who is seven. It's her hard shoes thumping angrily against the leg of my favorite dining room table. Her parents have brought her with them for Sunday lunch, and right now they look like they would like to disappear under the table with embarrassment at their child's behavior.

We always include our own children at the table, so they understand how to behave, and I can see their shocked glances as they gaze upon this scene. The other adults seem just as awkward and unsettled.

Charlotte, who has decided she doesn't want to eat the broccoli her parents served her, is putting up a strong defense against her father's attempted persuasion. Eventually, he loses his cool, bangs the table, and with a raised voice demands, "Just eat it now!" Everybody—including me—gets a bit of a fright at this harsh and sudden roar. Her mother can only make soft noises of conciliation that no one seems to notice. Charlotte's small face is screwed into a flushed, concentrated look of determined rebellion. I am trying with all my might to just shut up and let the parents parent, but I

Introduction

can see this is not going to end well. I feel for both the child and the parents, but this is not the time to solve the problems of the world. I take a long sip of my wine and breathe.

The other kids at the table, sensing some sort of impending doom, have gone very quiet. I quietly get up to fetch the dessert course, while behind me the table explodes into tears and recriminations. By the time I return, all is fairly quiet. Someone has removed the offending vegetable, and we all enjoy the rest of our meal. However, two things are uppermost in my mind. One is—naturally—that someone has to get the dents out of my table leg, and the other is a mixture of compassion and irritation with what happened. Although I empathize with their situation, I'm not sure that this child will be included in any future invitations to my home.

Parents with out-of-control children often find their choices very limited. This is probably not what they signed up for. No doubt they had rosy, romantic visions of a whole different parenting experience. But in reality, people stop inviting them over, eating out is a worry, as, indeed, is any excursion out of the home. Home life itself is often chaotic, school life is no better, and friends, grandparents, and acquaintances look on in judgment as the parents try desperately to do the right thing. It's a pressure cooker of frustration and disappointment for everyone.

As a parent and professional life coach, I have been helping families with similar problems for many years. Many parents have not experienced good parenting themselves. Perhaps their families were challenged in ways that mean they have internalized unhelpful behavior patterns themselves or are trying to do the opposite but that isn't working, either. Perhaps nobody modeled effective parenting to them. Maybe these are skills that most people actually need to learn upfront, or early on, but only realize it as the kids get bigger and things get out of hand.

But badly behaved children grow into socially challenged adults who struggle until they learn to fit in or get left out permanently on the sidelines. Learning how to be amongst other people, how to show respect for others on all levels, and to develop empathy that allows for kindness, mutual understanding, and compassion is key to being a successful human being.

Power, money, good looks, great brains, and all the trappings that go with these things will only get you part of the way. What's more, all of these external things are potentially temporary.

One of my favorite quotes by Clarence Thomas, an Associate Justice of the Supreme Court of the United States, is: *"Good manners will open doors that the best education cannot."* Regardless of your connections or knowledge, dignified and courteous behavior can be your greatest asset. And you can only buy or talk your way out of so much trouble before it catches up with you.

People will respond to how well they are treated. If they are left feeling respected and peaceful after being around another person, chances are they will be more inclined to respond in kind by being helpful, and so on. We all know the old saying that you catch more flies with honey than vinegar.

No matter what it is you do, how you do it makes the difference between success or failure. You can either live with style, kindness, grace, and good manners, or you can choose the other path. That path is much rockier and harder to traverse. It's also lonely.

The fact is, human beings live in a wider society. Those cute little bundles need to grow up and learn to get along in a variety of social situations, including school, work, friendships and more. What seems cute when they are small gets less so as they get bigger. As parents, we know we need to help them learn how to get along in all situations. We know that this is important to their success in life, but we ourselves don't always have the answers or know where to begin.

Introduction

We're often left asking where we are going wrong.

Looking at the broccoli episode, or the B.E., as my kids refer to it now, I'm sure some questions popped into your head. If you're an experienced parent with fairly well-behaved children, you probably spotted a few issues from a mile away. On the other hand, perhaps you have some similar problems yourself and really feel for these frustrated parents. If you're a new parent, you're probably shuddering at the thought of your future, or thinking smugly that your child would never behave like that. When it comes to a 'naughty' child, everyone likes to have an opinion. The fact is that opinions just put everyone on the defensive. They don't really help.

When faced with children who don't yet know how to behave in socially acceptable ways, we need to develop an attitude of curiosity before jumping in with solutions. What we know for sure is that every child comes with their own needs, challenges, likes, dislikes, abilities, and personality, as does each parent. Every family unit has its own dynamics, too. Everyone is at a different level of self-awareness, self-control, and understanding about what is okay or not okay.

What we also know is that parenting is hard. Often you are learning right alongside your kids. The challenges of modern lifestyles—complete with rapidly advancing levels of technology—means that parenting now is vastly different to 10 years, or a generation, ago. How we were raised is simply not the same as the challenges and dangers modern parents face.

Quite often a challenging family situation is no one's fault, per se. Take the Broccoli Family as an example. They are two working parents and get a few hours, at most, in the evenings and over weekends to practice their parenting. During those hours they also have homework, dinners, chores, and many other responsibilities to deal with. They haven't really thought about a consistent approach to discipline. It's all on the fly, and in their home it always feels a bit chaotic. The children pretty much do what they want, get overtired and overwhelmed, and act up, until invariably one of the parents explodes or just gives in. It's a mix of no parenting with fear-based parenting. Everyone's tired, and nobody is thinking about the future very much. It's a recipe for disaster, as those early schoolchildren and preteens will soon be older and tougher to handle.

Effective parenting isn't as simple as just forcing, or telling, bribing, yelling, manipulating, or worse. These are short-term solutions that mainly use fear to get results, and it doesn't yield the best results or build relationships, at least not long-term anyway. Anyone on the receiving end of this parenting style can tell you how it did not work for them and just broke them down in the end. These are generally not happy families, and years later, these parents will sit on their own wondering why no one ever visits.

It takes a smarter, more patient approach. It takes understanding of ourselves so we can understand our kids better. It's a journey we take together with our children, and in the end, we will all be better people for it, if we approach it right. I'm talking about discipline used constructively rather than destructively. Action that is positive, builds everyone up, and empowers children to be self-managing and responsible future members of the world.

We need to learn how to use positive discipline in a constructive way that gets everyone wanting to cooperate, even when we're not there to oversee things. Understanding how to behave in a way that works with and for others as well as yourself is a learned skill, and it comes with some foundational stuff like self-awareness, knowing how to communicate, and also to solve problems. Kids aren't born knowing any of this; we need to teach them.

You want the best for your children, of course. Most parents do. But to teach a thing, you need first to fully understand it. And you also need to understand what's going on in the hearts and

Introduction

minds of your precious bundles of joy, who are getting taller and more complex by the second.

I have walked this path myself. I have also stood by and walked alongside many families who have needed to grow and learn together as a whole unit to get this right. It is possible.

If you're reading this book, then you probably are more like the Broccoli Family than you would like. Believe it or not, there's no need to struggle. There are some fairly simple things you can start applying straight away that will ease the tension for everyone. That's the reason for this book. Happier, calmer families create happier, calmer people in general; at work, at school, and at home. It makes getting on with the bigger picture of life, like careers, learning, and living day-to-day, so much easier. It also grows more stable, balanced adults who in turn raise happier, calmer children themselves.

Let's take a look together at what might work for you.

1

Being Human

In a national survey on manners, the stats showed that 83% of children between 10 and 14 admitted they did not have great table manners, 41% did not know how to greet others politely, and 40% reported that they had used social media to say mean things about other people (Finesse Worldwide, 2019). While not knowing how to pass the salt isn't the end of the world, not knowing how to show courtesy, respect, or why kindness is important has a more sinister undertone.

It speaks to a lack of self-awareness, and also a shortage of empathy. If you aren't even aware of your problematic behavior, how can you fix it?

No or little empathy is a huge problem because without it we cannot function very well as a society. Empathy means being able to understand how others might be feeling. It enables you to see things from another person's perspective, to put yourself in their shoes to some degree. It helps us understand and interact better with each other. It also suggests that a person with empathy cares enough to notice when someone else is upset, miserable, or suffering. And if we understand and care, we're likely to want to do something about the problem.

> *"I believe empathy is the most essential quality of civilization."*
>
> Roger Ebert

Empathy helps build social connections, promotes helpful and prosocial behavior of all kinds, and links to compassion.

If that is missing, we end up with a hard, cruel world indeed; one where the weak are unprotected, suffering is ignored, abuse is okay, fear rules, and dog eats dog. That's not a world I'd like to live in.

Good manners are the end result of self-awareness, empathy, and socialization. They are the grease that helps turn the cogs of social interaction between the 7.753 billion people who live on the planet.

Ages and Stages

Just like you can't expect a fish to climb a tree, there are some things that are cognitively not possible before a certain age. In the old days, parents often treated children like small adults, but as our social and cognitive understanding has grown, thank goodness, people realized this wasn't the best approach.

Our brains develop and grow quite rapidly for the first 25 years of life. During this time, we can expect some behavior, as well as ability, to vary.

Being Human

Age	Attention span	Emotional ability	Emotional care
0-12 months	A few seconds at most. By one year this increases to a few minutes.	Attached to a primary caregiver. May be scared by strangers. Cries to get needs met.	Requires a responsive caregiver and a secure, loving environment or may learn unhealthy attachment strategies and become insecure and battle with trust later on. Childproof your home before they start to crawl.
12-24 months	One to four minutes.	Can be impatient and easily frustrated. Temper tantrums may be common. Has learned object permanence by now, which means they know you are coming back. Can understand 10 to 20 words. Can speak two or three words and adds to this slowly. Starts to imitate and copy behavior they see. Starts learning very basic toileting and self-care if encouraged.	Childproof your home if not already done. Make sure routines, healthy diets, and sleep schedules are in place. Model the behavior you want to see at later stages and repeat patiently. Give lots of gentle physical guidance, verbalize boundaries (what is okay and not okay or safe/unsafe) but still provide direct care.
2-6 years old	Four to 12 minutes maximum.	By two they have 50 words or more. As they learn more language and can communicate their needs, they calm down and are less frustrated. They start showing empathy and learning, sharing and taking turns. By six they have around 20,000 words. They can follow some simple instructions, do a few basic chores, follow more complex instructions, and do basic problem-solving. Have improved self-control and can maintain emotional stability.	Gentle reminders around the rules and boundaries will be needed. Establish predictable routines. Encourage regular playdates where they can learn to be around other children. A lot of social learning can happen through play. Be consistent with boundaries and modeling good behavior. Let them help with whatever simple chores they can; it gives them a sense of independence and encourages cooperation. Let them try to do stuff for themselves, like dressing, brushing teeth, and so on. Increase complexity as they show ability. Catch them doing 'right' and use a lot of praise.

6-12 years old	A maximum of 20 minutes before they have a lapse in attention and need to refocus.	They are learning conversational conventions like eye contact and greetings. Can do problem-solving and compromises. Have better emotional self-control. Able to do more complex household chores like tidying up, sweeping, and washing dishes.	Spend time talking and checking in with them daily. Keep teaching self-care, emotionally and physically. Remind about manners and boundaries, as needed. Include positive rewards for desired behavior. Discuss why unwanted behavior doesn't work and why. Let them tell you what consequences they should face for bad behavior. Don't stop with the hugs, cuddles, and games.
13-18 years		Along with shifts in hormones come some emotional behaviors. Brains are still developing and teens are often more risk-taking and adventurous but not often with an idea of real-life consequences. They are forming a sense of identity separate from you.	Keep privileges related to desired behavior. Give increased independence as they show increased responsibility. Social and emotional skills may still need some tweaking, reminding, and assistance. Keep communication as open as possible. Teach and model self-control and problem-solving strategies.
18-25 years		They are likely to seek out your opinion if you have established a strong relationship with them. Their brains are still developing but now their self-care is up to them more than not, so hopefully you have taught them well.	By 18 they are considered adults, and while they are responsible for themselves, they may still need some financial and lifestyle support. They should be moving towards financial independence of some sort. You are taking less of a parental role and more of a friendly and supportive one.

Common to all ages and stages, except perhaps the very young and young adults over 18, are certain things you can do to support your children with their emotional development, as well as their general socialization skills. While we will discuss all of these in more depth throughout the book, my formula for a well-socialized and happy kid includes:

- Being emotionally available to them, which also means you need to be working on yourself so that you can fulfill this need for them.
- Don't forget loads of physical touch, kisses, cuddles, games, laughing, chasing, dancing, jumping, and fun. Both both boys and girls need physical affection, at least

until they get to the age where that's no longer cool, and even then sneak in as many hugs as you can.
- Defining boundaries and clearly communicating and managing them with consistent consequences if they are overstepped. Decide what these are and be as consistent as possible, but also be aware that sometimes we need to adjust the rules if they are not working or put other support systems in place. Make the kids part of that conversation if they are old enough for it.
- Allowing your child increased responsibility and independence as they show an increase in ability to deal with it, and removing or adjusting it if that changes.
- Making sure your kids receive balanced nutrition and enough sleep.
- Making sure your kids get some sunshine and fresh air. Every day should include some level of physical activity, even if it's just walking the dog.
- Space to learn and play creatively. This includes some time for them to experience boredom, because boredom lets creativity awaken.
- Play loads of board games and family games from early on. Match the games to their ability, of course. This teaches turn-taking, problem-solving, and compromises.
- Sit down together for meals, and don't allow any devices at the table. This is how table manners are learned.
- Teach them responsible device usage. Show them how to self-regulate, for example, getting off a game if they start feeling grumpy or overwhelmed. Discuss safe social media use and etiquette, as well as handling cyber-bullying. After bedtime, and a good hour or so before, all devices should be off.
- Chances to interact with people of all ages and types, in a range of social settings, with you guiding and modeling correct behavior. They will learn how to interact with a diverse range of people and what is appropriate in

various age groups or for genders, and other cultural backgrounds. Such knowledge is invaluable. Teach them to respect (and expect) differences, as nobody thinks or feels exactly the same way. We are all unique.
- Chances to try things for themselves, struggle a little, and learn as a result. This means not peeling their fruit for them once they are able to, letting them make their own school lunches, pack their own bags, and also face the consequences of not doing what they needed to do. This is the only way they learn and grow empowered. Overprotection and doing everything for them limits their growth.
- Include them in the household chores and responsibilities. A toddler can sweep the floor, pack the vegetable bin, or pick up toys, even if it's not that great a job. A preschooler can load and unload the dishwasher, pick up dog poop, feed pets, vacuum, set the table, and so on. A school-aged child can help fold laundry, maybe even learn to do the laundry, and help with cleaning in general. Older kids can help with the shopping. These chores help them learn what it takes to live in the world, and also gives them a sense of pride and responsibility.
- Give them chances to help out. Volunteering their time and efforts at a pet shelter, old-aged home, or wherever else seems appropriate, even if you go with them at first, helps them learn empathy and gives them insight into other people's lives and needs. It also empowers them and helps them feel good.
- Let them wait for things when feasible, and delay gratification from time to time.
- Model how to deal with problems, resolve conflict, and regulate emotions in healthy ways. Don't hide the general, day-to-day issues from the kids. Let them see you dealing with stuff. Obviously keep this age-appropriate and don't make your child into your own

little emotional whipping bag or talk therapist for adult issues.
- Show them how to greet, say please and thank you, say goodbye, take turns, share, and to recognize when they have made a mistake and how to apologize.

This all amounts to a balanced lifestyle, including what kids need and not just what they want. As a parent, your primary responsibility is to ensure your children survive and learn how to fend for themselves once they leave the nest, but along with that go a lot of essential mental, emotional, and social skills.

How to Teach (and Learn) Self-Awareness

All positive mental, emotional, and spiritual growth starts with self-awareness. And that means being objectively aware of your thoughts, feelings, and actions. Once you have this awareness, it means you can start making more helpful choices for yourself and others. It's not easy for many adults, so how do we even start teaching it to children?

Depending on the age and stage of the child, you would obviously need to simplify accordingly, but a lot of the following actions can be taken with your kids from a fairly early age.

- *Name feelings.* Get in the habit of asking "How do we feel today?" You can even use emojis or a feelings chart (there are many online) to find the feeling of the moment. Giving children words for feelings helps them understand themselves better, and also helps them recognize those feelings in others.
- *Allow feelings to exist.* So often we avoid or push feelings away, and that doesn't help us to process or manage them. The funny thing is, until we process a feeling, it often comes back bigger and badder over and over again.

The root cause never gets dealt with, and we end up stuck and feeling bad a lot of the time, even if we don't want to admit it. Unacknowledged feelings can find other unhealthy outlets in anxiety, depression, substance abuse, and so on.

- *Talk and reflect about thoughts and feelings.* Our thoughts about a situation can be pretty negative or even faulty and missing some of the facts. If we can start watching the quality of our thoughts, we take a big step towards self-awareness. Our thoughts are what trigger our brains to react, releasing various chemicals that underlie emotions, whether this is anger, sadness, joy, connection, closeness, fear or any other feeling. When our feelings are off, we can learn to examine our thoughts and also consider the triggering situation to see what might be changed and improved upon. Teaching kids to see feelings as messengers of information about themselves is a key skill. It empowers them not to be ruled by feelings, too. Not every feeling is true or needs to be acted upon if we know how to allow and process feelings.
- *Look at our choices and how they link to our feelings.* When other people behave in certain ways, we can use this as a teachable moment. We can discuss what happened and what that person might be feeling. We can reflect on what they could have done differently or better.
- *Praise and reward their own good choices and reflect on what did not work so well.* Let them tell you rather than the other way around, or use lots of questions to open up their thinking about a situation.
- *Take the lesson.* If we find that something we said or did doesn't work out so well, what do we need to do more of or less of and how? Help your child put this into concrete, visible steps to do or not do.

- *Process and release bad feelings using movement* (exercise or activity of any sort), art, music, talking, nature, or journaling. This will help them to direct the energy of a feeling into something productive rather than something destructive. This helps us depressurize and feel calmer and more in control.
- When a choice has resulted in bad behavior and harm to others, *help your children reflect on what happened and their part in it*. Discuss how their actions made others feel and behave, and show them the cause and effect link in how a situation played out.
- *Learn how to give and receive feedback, starting with you.* While you can share your thoughts, it's a good idea to encourage them to also share theirs, too. Encourage a trusted mentor, such as a non-judgmental family member or friend, to be there for them. This gives them external input and someone who they can turn to for advice other than just you. When they do give you feedback on your own behavior, put aside your ego and listen fully. Apologize when you're in the wrong. By modeling this, you show them how to deal with critical input calmly and intelligently. This can include teaching them how to know when feedback is helpful and when it's not.

All of this adds up to teaching mental and emotional self-care, which is a vital skill. Before we can function out there in the world, we need to be okay inside ourselves first. And if we're not, we need to know what to do to get there.

Teaching Children About Boundaries

This is basically what is okay or not okay for those around us. Children need both to learn respect for other people's boundaries and also how to protect and set up their own.

In any social setting, whether at school or later on at work, we encounter a range of people who will all have their own likes, dislikes, and personal boundaries. Some of these people may be damaged or have learned unhealthy ways of being in the world, and by teaching your kids about boundaries early on, you help them protect themselves from this kind of negativity. Boundaries help deal with bullies, potential abusers, and also empower your child to know what they want and what they don't, and how to get that.

You can start discussing the following ideas with your children as soon as they are able to understand:

- When someone does or says mean things, or anything that makes you feel bad, you can say "no" and "stop." You can move away from them and, if you need to, you can ask another person (preferably an adult) for help.
- You can also tell your friends, teachers, and family if they're doing something you don't like because sometimes they won't realize. That way you can give them a chance to behave better around you. If you don't speak up, people won't always know how you feel. If they don't listen, you can move away from them and you can ask someone else for help.
- Always tell your parents (or a helpful mentor/adult that you set up as a neutral, safe space for them) if this happens so we can help you. Nobody can make you keep secrets that make you feel bad or confused.
- If someone says "no" or "stop" to you, you need to listen and move away from them. Again, talk to your parents or somebody helpful about what happened.
- Nobody has the right to come into your personal body space without your permission. (You can model what personal space is, and also discuss what to do if this happens.)

- Nobody has the right to do ugly, hurtful things to you or say mean, ugly words to you.
- Your boundary is like your own personal force field of protection. It's invisible and is made by you using words and actions. You decide when to turn it on and when it goes off. You are in control of it.
- You will mostly need to use your boundaries around people who make you feel bad. The people who normally make you feel happy and are good to be around will already know a lot about respecting your boundaries.

I find describing boundaries as a force field, or energy shield, helps most preschoolers and school-going kids understand and visualize what they are and what they are used for. Most kids have watched *Star Wars* or something similar and can relate to this. Otherwise, find words that relate to their interests. What do their heroes and heroines use to protect themselves?

Having an open discussion about what feels bad (to them) and what needs to change for that to stop can help them identify what their personal boundaries are and how to put them in place.

Remind them that:

- Noticing when a boundary is being crossed is important. When someone is doing this, it makes you feel bad, grumpy, upset, resentful, and sometimes even scared.
- It's important to listen and learn when people remind you to do the good things you need to be doing. That's how you become super awesome in life. Sometimes that can feel a bit bad, but it's not the same bad feeling as when someone is intentionally using, hurting, or being mean to you.
- Saying what you do and don't want or like is important so that people can know. People cannot read your mind.

- Boundaries go both ways. You need to respect other people and they, in turn, respect what you want.
- If people don't want to respect you, you don't need to be around them. You need to respect and look after yourself first. That is most important. It doesn't matter if someone says they don't like you after you have said "no." This kind of person would not make a good friend anyway.
- Adults can make mistakes, too. Grownups can do or say hurtful things, and that might mean that they still have some learning to do themselves. When people behave badly, it's normally because they have problems inside them that have nothing much to do with you.
- Always ask for help if you can't handle stuff on your own.

Older kids may need more of a reasoned discussion around these principles. You can discuss personal values (what's important to them) and talk about situations where they felt their boundaries were not being respected.

Before we look at the end result—the manners that we want our children to have—we need to take a few steps back to the root of the idea. In order to internalize how to behave in polite society, a few other building blocks should be in place first.

The sooner you can start building empathy, self-awareness, self-worth, and emotional self-management in your children, the better. But even if you come a bit late to the party, these are issues you can work on together as a family with older children. To increase understanding, build your kids up and encourage more appropriate behavior.

2

Teaching Manners

It's early in the morning and you haven't even had your first cup of coffee. It's been a long night, with lots of wake-ups, calls for water, and playing musical beds with your four-year-old. You're exhausted before you even start and already running late for work. You're just about to walk out the door when chaos erupts.

From the foyer, a huge crash and sound of breaking glass resounds. You race through to find your son standing barefoot in the middle of broken shards of that precious antique 18th-century vase your aunt gave you. Biting back your anger, you quickly lift him clear of the danger and start picking up the mess. No sooner have you sorted that out than you hear another crash from the kitchen and crying. What now! It seems like the little hooligan is on a rampage, and this time he's broken a plate and cup in the kitchen.

Is he doing this on purpose? This is getting to be a habit. What's going on? By this age, he should know better, shouldn't he? Is he trying to anger you? All these thoughts race through your mind, and another stressful day starts off on the wrong foot for both of you.

Parenting can be super challenging. Most parents would flip out in a scenario like this. If they have the time and patience, they might discover that the child is trying to be helpful, and that these were just unfortunate accidents. On the other hand, they might discover that he did it all on purpose just to get your attention. And perhaps there is a reason for that, too.

When kids behave badly, we need to do our job as parents to help them improve, right? But to do that, we first have to be in control of ourselves. We should aim to get to the root cause of the behavior because nothing exists in a vacuum. And we have to teach them the skills they require to do better.

If you're reading this, you want your kids to be the best they can be. You want them to succeed in life and do well in a wide array of social settings that will help them towards this success. You likely want them to have happy, fulfilled, and meaningful lives.

As a parent or caregiver, one of your roles is that of guide and teacher. But not all of us know how to go about doing that. We may have experienced some pretty negative, harsh discipline ourselves and not know any other way to approach this with our own kids.

That's okay; these skills are learned, just like everything else. The thing to keep in mind is that if you want to instill long-term constructive behavior in your child, the most effective way to do so is constructively and positively.

Nobody ever in the history of the world changed their behavior through being beaten, forced, yelled at, criticized, and broken down. That might get immediate results, but everything reverts when your back is turned. Later there may be an uprising, revolution, or rejection of the person or people who thought they held the power. No helpful lessons are learned that way except to be fearful of you, avoid you and hide things from you.

You have to deal with inappropriate or destructive behavior, but you also need to do it in a way that doesn't break the child down, damage their self-worth, or destroy their confidence. Anything causing shame, degradation, humiliation, or lessening of the child's spirit is right out. In fact, acts and words like these are commonly referred to in discussions about child abuse. This abuse, whether verbal, emotional, or physical, only creates problems that your child will end up facing later in their lives as parents, partners, or just in their day-to-day lives. Things like anxiety, depression, lack of self-worth and self-control, and becoming bullies or abusers themselves all are in the cards if this is the parenting style they've been subjected to.

Most of us don't intentionally want that reality for our children's future. So, regardless of our own experiences with our parents, we need to break the cycle and approach this with the end goal of happy, healthy, balanced, and stable future adults in mind.

Positive discipline involves:

- *Taking the time to do the work.* A few extra minutes spent calming a baby can mean that that child will not grow up insecure or avoidant. Being responsive to early needs rather than ignoring them teaches the child to feel secure, to trust and how to relate to others better later. After infancy, taking the time to parent in the moment it's needed, and finding teachable moments along the way, adds up to less time spent in school disciplinarians' or therapists' offices later. I call this smart parenting. Take the time now to make more free time for yourself—and less stress—later.
- *Clearly and consistently stating the "rules" in age-appropriate ways the child can understand.* To be able to do this, you need to know what the rules are and why they are there. And if a rule isn't working, you have to be smart enough to change it. You also need to explain the

"why" so that people know what the point of it all is. Even little children need to know both "what" and "why" to help them understand and do what is needed.
- *Explain what the consequences are of breaking the rules.* Choose consequences that are non-destructive and less personally harmful like:

a. A temporary loss of a privilege. Removing desired objects like toys or devices for a set time. Canceling a favorite activity for a set time, or not allowing attendance at desired events.

b. You break it, so you must fix it. This could mean picking up toys that have been chucked around, cleaning up a mess, or making an apology.

c. Time out where they can cool off and calm down.

d. Redirect and distract them. At times, bad behavior comes from boredom or because they don't know what to do with themselves. Calmly state the rule, and then give them something to do. For example, "We do not throw and break things. Please go get the broom so we can sweep up."

Be consistent with applying the rules. I find letting children choose their own consequences can be very effective. Often they will choose much harsher ones than you would have, and then you can step in and dial back the consequences a bit. You win on two levels here. First, you appear reasonable and caring, and second, when they choose the consequence, they are more accepting of it.

- *Hearing your child out and asking lots of questions when a problem situation arises.* Get all the facts before you jump in with discipline or answers. This teaches them problem-solving skills too.

- *Watch out for the behavior you want and reward that.* This is called positive reinforcement.
- *Sometimes no response is the best response.* If they aren't doing anything dangerous, and they get lots of positive attention for good behavior, withdrawing your attention might be more effective in some situations. For example, your child is throwing their cookies off their high chair. Eventually, the cookies will run out, and if you don't pick them up, the child will have, in effect, disciplined himself. If a toy is broken, there is no more toy. If homework isn't done, they have to face the teacher tomorrow. Kids quickly learn to stop undesirable behavior when the natural consequences are allowed to unfold.
- *Walking your own talk.* The rules need to apply to you, too. If you want your child to be calm and kind, then you need to be that person too. If you're an angry, hard person, you are modeling anger and harshness, and that's what they will learn and reflect back at you and others.
- *Take a look at the environment.* If you live in a house full of breakable antique vases all left at toddler level, you are really asking for trouble. Keep in mind what the child is capable of and take action to make the environment more child-friendly. Just as you childproof your home when they are crawling about, you need to run a critical eye over your home, their school, and any other environments they find themselves in. Is there anything making it harder for them to behave well?

a. The physical environment needs to be set up for ease of use. Potential dangers or risks need to be removed and controlled.

For little kids, this might mean removing breakables and practicing safety in the home in general. This can extend into teen years, for example you make a teen den where they can be messy and watch their favorite TV shows in a space it won't affect the adults. Perhaps this might mean curfews, GPS trackers, and other teen-level guidelines to deal with their more independent context and still keep them safe.

b. The mental and emotional environment needs to be supportive and safe.

- *Plan ahead*. Sometimes you know that certain situations will arise and so you can be more mentally prepared for it.

Practical Exercise: Planning for Trouble

Take some time to consider your children, their ages, and diverse needs, and then answer the following questions:

1. What are the current behaviors that aren't working for you or others? Write these down in a list.
2. What are the kinds of things you can expect to happen now and down the line? It might help to do a bit of research, chat to friends with kids, join an online parenting group, and also simply brainstorm this a bit.
3. How likely is it for each of these things to happen? Rate it 1 to 3, with 1 being unlikely and 3 being very likely. The unlikely stuff you can deal with last, if at all.
4. For the very likely events, what would the best positive parenting response be?
5. What might make this difficult, or what extra support and resources might you need? Who or what can be of assistance? Who or what is making the situation worse, and what can you do about that?
6. What other steps can you take to avoid, reduce, or redirect unwanted behavior? List them as things you can get ready, things you can do right now, and things that

need more time or other resources to do. That way, you can prioritize them more easily.

Staying Calm

Managing your own reactions is key to managing child behavior.

How do we do this? A quick biology lesson is normally enough.

When you are scared or angry, your fight-or-flight response kicks in. Your brain triggers your body to release adrenaline and other stress chemicals to help you deal with whatever action you need to take. Back in primeval times, this was fine, because you were mostly running away from, fighting, or hiding from danger.

You know you're in this state because you clench your hands, jaw, and other muscles. You may shake, sweat, or feel nauseous, unsettled, and generally rattled. These are the fight-or-flight chemicals increasing blood flow, releasing extra sugars, cutting off non-essential body functions like digestion, and getting you ready to fight, run, or hide. In this state, your animal brain is in control, and odds are, you will not make the best, logical choices in more complex situations that don't require any of the above. Complicated problem-solving is out the window.

While we still have this programmed into us, it is not so useful when it comes to everyday modern life. It tends to make us more reactive than constructively responsive.

So, the first trick of good parenting is to learn how to calm your body so that you can use your higher thinking rather than your animal brain that wants to fight, attack, hurt, or run away.

It's pretty simple. If at all possible, delay your response and give the stress chemicals time to work their way out of your system:

- Leave the room or the area, if feasible. If the child is old enough, you can tell them you will be coming back to

discuss the issue later, when you're calmer. This models good self-control, by the way.
- Breathe it out. Slow counting and breathing is a great way to calm yourself quickly.
- Use an activity of any sort to work the chemicals out of your system, something mildly physical like a quick household chore or walking the dog can be effective for this.

If you cannot stay calm and well-behaved, how can you expect your child to do so? You need to be better than them at this, because you're their teacher, their safe anchor, and their role model.

Be Clear, Heard, and Understood

When you're calm and ready to deal with the situation, now you're ready to talk.

Get down on the child's level and make eye contact. This helps you connect to them, and them to you, for better mutual understanding.

Keep your body relaxed and your voice calm. If you're stressed, your voice tends to go up in tone as your vocal chords constrict. Research shows that children hear and respond to lower, deeper voices better than high shouting or whining ones.

Be clear on your end goal, and keep it in mind when you say whatever it is you need to say. Remember:

- Keep it clean. No mean words from your side, otherwise, what are you modeling?
- Keep it behavior-focused and not personal. In other words, say, "I don't like this situation/event" rather than

"you are a bad kid." If you make it personal, the child takes those labels on. They think, "oh well, I'm a bad kid" and they have less reason to try or do better in that case.
- Share the negative input their behavior is having on others and how that makes them feel (or you, if you are the one being impacted).
- Be firm but constructive. How can the child do better?
- Let them give input and listen.
- Be clear on what is expected going forward. Make it SMART (specific, measurable, achievable, realistic, and time-framed).
- Be clear on future consequences.

For example:

You say, "*We do not break stuff on purpose.*

We leave special stuff belonging to other people alone (like the vase), and we ask for help if we need it.

I feel really upset and sad that I have to clean up this mess and my best vase is broken. I really liked that vase. It was special to me. I was also worried because you could have cut your feet on the glass and hurt yourself. You might have been bleeding and needed to go to the doctor."

(It helps to be specific and use sensory images like this, as kids dial into it if they can picture the consequences well.)

"*What happened?*"

Child says, "*Sorry, Daddy, I wanted to look at the vase, and then I was trying to help clean up in the kitchen.*"

(This puts the whole thing in perspective, doesn't it? He wasn't being intentionally naughty. He was probably trying to make up for breaking the vase by tidying the kitchen for you. Imagine if you had screamed and shouted at him and called him "bad"? Yikes!)

You say, *"Next time you want to look at something special, please ask me first. In the kitchen, and with plates and glasses, carry things one at a time and walk slowly and carefully, or ask for help, okay?*

I will know you're doing better when you stop breaking things like this. But next time you touch one of my special things without asking me, I'll take away one of your special toys.

Now what did I just say?"

(The child repeats it back so that you know he knows.)

"Why did I say this?"

(The child explains why you have this rule. Hopefully he understands. If not, repeat why you don't want him to do that thing again.)

"And what will you do next time?"

(The child tells you and hopefully this shows he understands. If not, help him a bit more.)

All of this may take you an extra few minutes, making you even later for work, but it's time well spent. Down the line, you'll need to spend much less time on this kind of issue, or similar ones, because you took the time for the lesson to be properly internalized by your child. In fact, he may never forget this moment and tell you one day how he remembers what happened.

Watch Your Words

When bringing a problem behavior to a child's attention, be aware of the kinds of words you use. People tend to overreact when they get a fright, or when they're angry. Then the wrong kinds of words can come pouring out. The problem is, these words can cause lasting damage.

1. Always ask: Is what I'm about to say kind, is it useful, and is it necessary? What will I achieve with my words? Always keep that in mind.
2. Be clear with your words, and check if the child understands what you said. Get their attention first before you speak.
3. Focus your words on a positive action. By this I mean focus on what you want them to do, and not what you don't want them to do. The reason for this is simple neuroscience and brain wiring. We focus on the main subject and verb of a sentence, and what we focus on happens. So if you say: "Don't knock your water glass over," odds are, all the child's brain hears is "Knock your water glass over." Hey presto! A few minutes later the glass gets knocked over and everyone is upset.
4. Be mindful that the labels and negative words you use can stick in that child's head for a very long time. In my middle age I still remember clearly things said to me as a child, especially the things that hurt and harmed me. If I go back to that adult and discuss it, they don't even remember saying that stuff and never meant it that way. Those negative words are often internalized by the child and played back again and again whenever anything goes wrong for them. They become a negative inner voice that is very destructive. Kids are very open to, unprotected from, and absorbent of all things said and done around them in those first years. That's why so many therapists want to know about your childhood, because it can define the rest of your life. Keep that in mind when parenting.

There will be times when you want to explode, or you're tested beyond your abilities when parenting. You won't always get it right because nobody does. But you can do your best and reflect often on what is going right, or what you need to do less of. Being a self-aware, mindful parent is one of the best gifts you can give your kids.

3

Basic Manners

It's all very well to talk about good manners, but what actually are they? Each family unit will have their own way of doing things, and each person has their own unique set of boundaries, so this can be a little complicated. Times have changed, and so have lifestyles and expectations.

Also, what constitutes good manners in this country may be considered atrociously rude in another. What is acceptable in a gang of guys may not be acceptable when in a mixed group, and what's fine with your friends may be horribly wrong when talking to your great-aunt Martha. You know, the one who sent you that vase.

Manners can vary, and many old-school manners are no longer expected. However, if you do get them right, you'll be remembered as being impeccable in your behavior.

While good manners might not be considered that important by younger generations, that could well be a result of working parents who haven't had the time to properly teach their children. The use of devices means less social interaction and less understanding of how to interact with people in person. There are just more people in the world, along with technology reinforcing distraction and instant gratification, immoral and unmannered role models, and so on.

But don't think this is anything new. Ours is far from the first society to complain about bad-mannered kids. It seems every generation looks at the ones coming after with a little bit of shock and surprise. Socrates, a Greek Philosopher from over 2,000 years ago, said children *"have bad manners, contempt for authority; they show disrespect for elders…and are now tyrants"* (Lipson, 2019).

However, all of this aside, there are some general, more universal guidelines that may apply to most people.

Pleases and Thank Yous

Acknowledging the things people do for you is useful if you want them to continue doing it. A simple "please" or "thank you" goes a long way towards greasing the social wheel of reciprocity.

When asking for something, no matter what it is, always preface the request with "please." It shows respect for the other person. Leaving it out can make the listener feel defensive or insulted.

Once something has been done for you, no matter what it is, a "thank you" shows that you have noticed and appreciate their efforts. This extends from small acts, like someone making you a cup of tea or holding open a door for you, to larger ones, like being taken for a meal, or having a lovely day out.

You can teach little kids this simple nicety from the time they start talking, even if they can't say it fully or properly at first. By modeling the words every time you want them to do something, and also whenever they have successfully attempted or completed a wanted behavior, it becomes second nature for them, too.

Another important form of "thank you" is found in the thank-you card. This is typically handwritten and sent after birthday parties or other events where a gift has been given to you. Get your children in the habit of doing this as soon as they can hold a crayon, even if at first it's just a meaningless squiggle with a picture they draw.

Friendliness

An open, friendly face with a smile is the foundation to putting others at ease. In some cultures, like Russia, too much friendliness may be seen as suspicious. In Japan and Iran, it's also not a straightforward sign of friendliness but is slightly more acceptable.

However, in most places in the world, a genuine smile that shows in your eyes is a way to show respect and friendliness, even to total strangers or to people who are serving you in retail stores, restaurants, and other venues.

Smiling and nodding are both ways to acknowledge the existence of another human being.

The amount of friendliness shown is usually relative to how well you know a person. The better you know them, the more friendly you may be expected to be.

Apologizing

This is a biggie. Many of us don't know how to make a real apology, or do it grudgingly.

If we've made a mistake, inconvenienced or caused any level of damage to another, an apology is the best way forward. The only time it isn't is when seeing or speaking with you will cause more harm than good. But that's probably reserved for some pretty serious bad behavior.

In most cases, the advised formula is:

1. Check that it's okay to apologize. If now isn't a good time, ask when a better time would be.
2. Make sure you're clear on what you did wrong. If you're not, and the other person is willing, ask them to explain how they feel and what the results of your actions were so that you can fully understand. Don't argue or tell them they're wrong about any of this. Only they will know how they feel and the impact of the situation on them.
3. Say sorry, and then explain exactly what you are sorry for and why you believe it was wrong.
4. State what you will do differently going forward. And then be sure to actually do that. An apology means very little if it doesn't result in changed behavior. If you make a habit of that, after a while people will stop believing your apologies.

Teach this formula and the understanding behind it to your kids from as early as possible. Use questions and guide them through the steps each time they need to say sorry until they get it. Let them tell you what they need to do next, and if they're struggling, make suggestions to help them along. By age four, most kids can say sorry and understand and mean it.

When you make mistakes with your children—and you surely will—be sure you also reciprocate and apologize, if needed. This models the correct behavior and shows them that you respect them too.

Gossiping

Gossiping is an insidiously bad habit. It can seem fun to dish out all the dirt and share the spicy secrets and personal affairs of others. Some people do this so they can feel important and be the center of attention. But they're paying for this using other people's currency.

In reality, gossip is never good. Anyone listening may respond with interest, but they will also be judging the gossiper. Clearly, this person is not safe to share any intimate details with and can't be trusted.

Teach your children the difference between sharing useful information and sharing gossip. If you catch them gossiping, ask them how they would feel if they knew others were talking about them in that way. Ask them if they could say these things in front of the person about whom they are talking.

Also teach the zen "three gates" of talking to or about others.

1. Is it true?
2. Is it necessary to say this?
3. Is it kind?

If what is to be said does not pass all of these gates, don't say it. We may not always get this right, but we can make a good attempt to and stay mindful of the quality of our words.

Sharing and Taking Turns

This is a tricky one and often misapplied in an attempt to teach sharing to young kids. I have seen little kids forced to "share" by having their favorite toys taken away and given to another child, and that's not helpful. It only teaches them that people can take stuff away from them and they have no rights or say in the matter.

First of all, kids only understand sharing properly around the age of four. Before that, an unwillingness to share is fairly normal. And to be honest, I know plenty of adults who don't wish to share and don't do so.

When teaching sharing, make sure that:

- There are plenty of toys or other resources of a similar nature for all the children present. Otherwise, put them away.
- Your child's favorite and treasured objects are not included in what needs to be shared. If you know other children will be present, it may be a good idea to put this stuff away for the duration.
- For children under three-and-a-half, be sure to have a few distractions on hand if the sharing goes awry. Have another activity, set of toys, or game that you can focus upset toddlers on if it all goes pear-shaped.
- You don't force sharing. But also, don't allow one child to hog all the things, either. If no one can cooperate, then remove the desired objects from all the children and distract them with new stuff.

Model sharing and taking turns with your child using age-appropriate games that you play with them.

Taking turns is learned through play such as hide-and-seek, ball games, racquet-and-ball games, cards, board games, and games like Jenga, Pick Up Sticks, and similar. It's a good idea to spend some time playing turn-taking games with your child before you expect them to be able to apply this skill with others.

Being on Time

When an event of any kind has a start time, the polite thing to do is to arrive a few minutes before. Too early can be as impolite as too late. This is especially true for catered events, but learning to respect other people's time is an important lesson all around.

Time can be considered more valuable than anything else, as once it's gone, you can never get it back. It's a part of your life wasted if someone has kept you waiting unnecessarily. People who are habitually late for everything, for whatever reason, are in essence showing a fundamental disrespect for anyone else who is on time. There are many reasons (and excuses) given for those who always run late, but it's entirely possible to be on time with some basic time management skills. You can teach these to your children as they grow, together with the basic idea that being on time is the respectful thing to do.

- Plan your week and day ahead so you know what's coming up. Use a diary, calendar, or app to help you remember your commitments. Keeping a colorful, centrally visible (like in the kitchen or hallway) family calendar is helpful when teaching this concept to your children. It's also particularly useful when you have more than one child and when school starts, as things quickly get complicated.
- When you make a time commitment, put it into your time system as soon as possible, as it's easy to forget otherwise.
- Allow additional time for things you know are variable and/or outside of your control such as taxis, other people, time to get ready if you have smaller children, and so on.
- If you are running late for any reason, let the others know. Apologize when you arrive.

It's better to arrive slightly earlier and spend that time doing something constructive than too late.

Pets

Your beloved animal friends may be your world, but they aren't necessarily loved as much by everyone. In your home environment, you will no doubt allow your pets to do whatever it is you feel is okay in your own space. Bear in mind that if you invite people to your home, they will not want to be jumped on, scratched, or otherwise have their space invaded by your pets.

If your pets are not well trained and likely to jump or otherwise harm a visitor or their belongings, either don't have visitors or put your pets safely away before anyone arrives. I know some people who say their pets are their babies and they can do whatever they like in their own home. I simply don't visit those people, as it's just too unpleasant if the animals are out of control.

Pet etiquette is even more important when taking them out into the public domain. Other people have a right to enjoy public areas and remain safe doing so without being worried about your pets.

It comes down to what level of training and control you have, and what potential danger your pet could be. Dogs, for example, should always be leashed if there is any doubt whatsoever, and often public areas require this or don't allow pets at all.

If your pet messes in a public area, it's your responsibility to clean it up, too. It's because of irresponsible pet owners that many areas now have no pets allowed policies, or very strict rules.

Bear in mind some people have had traumatic animal attack experiences or are just scared, so don't downplay these very real fears. Most often, if your pet misbehaves in a public domain, you will be held responsible, legally and otherwise.

Take your children along to pet training classes, if possible, so they can understand how animals behave and respond and how to control their own pets. When in public with your pet, model the polite and correct pet etiquette and encourage your children to be part of that, too.

Conversations

From day one you will be having some form of conversation with your baby. Smiling, gurgling, and taking turns to make baby noises or use full words with each other teaches a baby the beginnings of conversation.

As your child gets bigger, you can refine this. Encourage them to:

- Take turns and wait their turn to speak. Check that people are finished speaking before speaking themselves.
- Listen when other people are speaking, then respond appropriately, if a response is required.
- Show a real interest, as much as possible, or politely excuse themselves from an unwanted conversation.
- Not shout or interrupt others.
- Say "excuse me" if they have a valid reason to get immediate attention.
- Speak clearly. Especially as they get bigger, some kids have a tendency to speak too fast or to look at their shoes and mumble. It may take constant, gentle reminders, and perhaps even elocution lessons, to get them to communicate better. Drama training is always a great way to build confidence and clarity.
- Pay attention during a conversation they are a part of. No cellphones or other distractions are to be used. These need to be laid face down, or put away.
- Look at the person speaking and remove sunglasses so that some eye contact can be made.
- Pay attention when people share their names, and make an effort to remember these names. Using a person's name a few times after an introduction is one way to set it into memory, as is rhyming the name with something else, or matching it with a mental picture of some sort.

- Stop or alter the direction of a controversial, gossipy, nosy, invasive, or inappropriate topic. Teach them a range of options to use to deflect or stop a conversation they do not wish to be a part of. This comes back to having good boundaries.

Polite conversation is the bedrock of most human interaction. People who do not know how to apply these basics often unwittingly offend others, and may find they are avoided, or even socially rejected, because they can't hold a simple conversation in a polite way.

Conversational skills, whether face to face or over the phone, help build relationships and social inclusiveness. Most children should be able to conduct a simple conversation by the age of six at the latest. Gentle reminders and modeling this with them will help them get there.

Dress for Success

Dress codes have relaxed a lot over the last couple of generations. These days, an invitation will specify a dress code, if required, but in general, when in the public eye, it's best to:

- Cover vast expanses of skin like midriffs, belly buttons, and so on. When kids become teens they may challenge this, but you can teach them how to dress to suggest rather than reveal too much, if sex appeal is what they're going for. Mystery is always better than the naked truth when it comes to most public situations, regardless of what their favorite social media star might be doing.
- If attending a sport or summery, casual event, shorts, short skirts, and strappy tops are acceptable. Beachwear and swimwear depend on where you are in the world. If in doubt, always check. In some countries, for example,

it's considered extremely rude not to cover your head, or to expose various parts of the body, and you can even be fined or charged with a criminal offense. This is not so strict for small children, but as the parent, consider both the age and the level of respect required for any specific setting. For example, seeing a mostly naked baby in a shopping mall isn't everyone's cup of tea, apart from basic hygiene issues.

- Keep underwear underneath outerwear.
- Be clean and neat.
- If in doubt, dress smart casual. This means trousers, or a longer skirt, and a button-shirt or neat, fairly modest top, with closed or smart shoes.
- Unless you're going to a dress-up or pajama party, keep PJs for home wear.

Rightly or wrongly, the truth is that people will always judge you by what they see. A first impression is made in the time of an eye blink, based on what is seen. This happens before anyone has a chance to speak, so your appearance does matter.

Greeting and Departing

Just like we teach "please" and "thank you," saying "hello" and "goodbye" should be demonstrated and encouraged from early on.

On arriving anywhere, even at home or when seeing your family after a night's rest or a few hours of being busy elsewhere in the home, a simple acknowledgment of their presence is considered both polite and respectful.

This can be a "hello," "hi," or "good morning/day/afternoon," and may also include a query as to how the other person is doing in general.

The same applies when leaving for any period of time. "Goodbye," "good day," "good night," and so on, are all perfectly acceptable.

In these pandemic times, handshakes are no longer encouraged, but if you are ever in a position to give one, grasp the person's hand gently yet firmly, do not squeeze, and shake once.

Greet everyone in the room when you arrive and when you leave, unless doing so would disturb someone busy speaking. In which case, wait for them to finish and then do so, if at all possible.

Introductions

When a new person arrives, and the people already present don't all know this person, introductions are required. This is usually the responsibility of the host or hostess, or the person who has brought the new person into the space.

If you arrive somewhere and there's no one to introduce you, then in most circumstances it's acceptable to introduce yourself by name and politely greet the others.

Out and About

Whether or not you will ever see any of these people again in your life, the manner in which you move through life will be noted, and this will either work for you or against you. You never know who's watching, or which stranger you might need to ask a favor from at any given moment.

Not only that, how you treat people in general speaks volumes about the kind of person you are and will translate into how you behave in general. A person who is rude to strangers or service people will likely be rude to everyone on some level, or if not, then not trustworthy or authentic.

The types of behavior you can model for your children, and also encourage in them, include:

- Being patient and friendly with people in general in an appropriate manner.
- Being patient and friendly with any service staff, like waiters, retail assistants, and so on. Tipping any good service when it's received.
- Letting people off an elevator before you get on it.
- Letting people enter or depart before you through a door and holding the door for them if necessary.
- Letting someone with one or two items in front of you in the shopping queue.
- Observing and assisting anyone who is clearly struggling. Like an elderly person who has fallen or someone who can't reach a high shelf or open a door.
- Not grooming oneself in public. Things like putting on make-up, brushing hair (or teeth), picking ears (or noses) are best kept for in private. Even adjusting underclothes (or the bits in them) needs to be done somewhere private. Blowing one's nose into a tissue or handkerchief is okay, but then the proceeds need to be politely folded and put away. This also includes bodily functions like burping and farting. It's astounding how many people walk around unconsciously doing these things and, quite frankly, grossing out most people who are forced to experience it.
- No "manspreading" when in public. This means that you sit with your legs together and not taking up all the space.
- Offering up a seat on public transport to anybody who looks ill or weak, the elderly, or pregnant. Those who are better able should stand and let the weaker, more vulnerable people and those in clear need rest.

- If you need to ask a stranger for directions or other assistance, use a polite "excuse me" to get their attention. If they show willingness to assist, proceed with your request. Some people may be rushed or rude and ignore or brush you off, but that doesn't mean you need to lower yourself to their poor standards.

The presence of manners seems to decrease the more people are crowded into a limited area when, in fact, this is the time you all have to get along well even more than usual. Teaching your children to pay extra attention to manners when in public will create a general air of respect, kindness, and sociability that will benefit them throughout their lives and help them to get on well with others. The very act of being well-mannered can be quite rewarding in itself as it is, in essence, a form of service to others and the greater social structure. Even if others don't reciprocate, you always know that you behaved well, and that's a good feeling.

Doors

Respect for other people's privacy is a big one, especially in a larger family. Who wants someone to just burst in on them in their private space? Absolutely no one! It's private for a reason, and you don't know what you might walk in on.

Teaching little kids to close the door when they go to the bathroom (although perhaps take all keys out of doors when they are little to avoid lock-in accidents) and to respect a closed door can start as soon as they are walking about. Knocking on a closed door, asking for permission to come in, and respecting a "no" are vital parts of respecting other people's boundaries.

By the age of about six, children will have a good idea of what privacy means and start also wanting their own. As they express this need, be sure to discuss and agree on what it is so that you can demonstrate the concept by respecting the privacy they now would like to have.

Up until that age, parents might consider keeping their bedroom door closed when necessary, and gently but firmly reminding any kids that cross that boundary what the required behavior is.

It's also important to respect any closed doors in public spaces. When you demonstrate this to your children, do three knocks at most, and then wait for a response. If you don't get one, you should stop knocking and withdraw, as the person may be busy in a meeting or on a call or other private matter.

When arriving at the door of a friend, neighbor, or anyone else, a similar procedure is the norm.

Invitations

When invited to an event or to someone's home, the following is generally considered acceptable:

- Always respond to an invitation in good time, preferably in writing. For events, parties, or any catered affair, responding as soon as possible is advised and definitely a few days before, at the latest.
- Don't withdraw or attend at the last minute without a very good reason. It's extremely inconsiderate and impolite not to attend when you have given your reply as attending, and vice versa. In this case, a sincere apology would go a long way, but repeat offenders are unlikely to keep getting invited.
- Always ask before bringing a guest who wasn't on the original invitation. Confirm if the invitation allows for a guest, and whether you will or will not be bringing one.

- If you're invited to stay over in someone's home for the night, a small guest gift is generally appropriate to give them before leaving.
- Taking flowers or other small gift, like a bottle of wine, to a dinner event is also appropriate.
- For events at a person's home, you may wish to ask if there is anything further you can bring to contribute to the occasion. Sometimes hosts are grateful for extra food dishes, desserts, or bottled drinks, and other times they will be fully prepared and likely tell you to just bring yourselves.
- When in someone's home, or at a public event, apply the same norms of behavior as if you were in public, unless your host specifies otherwise. Pay attention to protecting their house rules and belongings. Use a coaster if you have a drink at a table. Let them know if something breaks and offer to replace it.

You won't be taking your children to many formal events in the early years, but there may be times when they are included. Obviously, some of the above is irrelevant for little kids under the age of six or so. However, once they reach this age, you can start discussing these forms of behavior and demonstrating it for events like party invites and playdates.

Family Events

These tend to be less formal than other invitations, but it obviously depends on the occasion. Family events are a great way to model to children how to behave in the wider world.

For family events, you still need to:

- Reply in good time.
- Check what to bring, if anything.

- Be on time.
- Advise on any changes in good time, if possible.
- Respect the rules of the person's home.
- Bring a small gift or token of appreciation.

While families can be informal, that doesn't mean that the host or hostess won't appreciate your good manners. Those closest to us will appreciate it even more when we treat them with the respect, kindness, and care we give to strangers.

Playdates and Parties

When invited for a playdate or party, your children will usually be expected to meet age-appropriate norms. Older children will definitely be expected to be able to control their behavior and respect the rules of the home being visited.

Birthday parties require that a nice outfit is worn and that a birthday present is taken and handed to the parents or birthday boy or girl. The value of the gift should not be an issue but rather the thought that has gone into it. When you're hosting the party, it's acceptable to leave the opening of the gifts until later to avoid smaller kids breaking them or any potential sharing issues.

On arriving and leaving, the usual greeting or farewell etiquette applies. Your child should, if old enough, personally thank the parents of their friend for the playdate or party and any special treats they had before they leave.

Play dates and parties normally require that the visiting parent stay for the duration of the playtime if the children are younger or the parents are meeting each other for the first time. Only once all the parents are comfortable that they know each other well enough are children left to the other adults' care.

A big no-no is leaving your child at a playdate or party and fetching them after the agreed collection time. Some parents use these events as babysitting opportunities, and I've had kids at my home up to four hours after a party has ended with no phone call or apology, much to my great dismay. Of course, although it is not the child's fault, their parents' lack of manners means they likely would not be invited again.

Table Manners

A lot of parents bemoan the fact that their children have no table manners. But, like with every sort of behavior, they need to be taught, modeled, and practiced frequently if children are to internalize them.

Where possible, what works best is to eat together as a family and include your children from as young as possible. This won't always make for restful dinners but will mean that you're not faced with a major problem down the line.

Some ways we have found, as a family, that we can all enjoy a peaceful family mealtime include:

- Doing family mealtimes when it's just us and no visitors.
- Doing family mealtime every day, when possible.
- Setting the table with cutlery and all the required bits and bobs and sitting at the table together, at the same time.
- Keeping to a set time, where possible.
- Not rushing.
- Not allowing any devices at the table, not even for the grownups.
- Using child-friendly place settings with plastic plates and stick-in-place, suction-bottom sippy cups, plus safe plastic cutlery for younger kids.
- Using clip-on chairs for children under three.
- Allowing a small toy for kids under two, if the food is not enough of a distraction.

- Allowing smaller children to leave when they clearly have had enough to eat and are getting extra wiggly. We made sure to keep a basket of toys in the corner of the dining area and childproofed the space so that our babies could not go far, and we could finish our meals in relative peace with them in eyesight if not at the table.
- Not forcing food a child does not like on them, and providing a choice of foods. When they're old enough, let them serve food for themselves. This avoids food tussles. Never insist the child clean their plate every meal (especially if they didn't serve themselves or choose the food items), as it can trigger serious emotional eating disorders later in life. I've learned that if a child has access to a variety of food over a few days, they will generally have a balanced diet. It's also not essential that they eat every vegetable, especially if they're getting some veggies or also eat fruit as part of their diet. A clever mom I know used reverse psychology on her stubborn kid. She stopped dishing him up any vegetables and only put them on her plate. When he asked why, she said, "These are only for grownups." Eventually, when she let him have some again, he was super keen. In my experience, giving little kids a variety of foods, especially finger foods, and doing baby-led weaning makes the whole vegetable thing a non-issue for most kids.
- Not overreacting to dropped food, knocked glasses, and so on. Simply get the child to help tidy up later, if they're old enough. Kids are still learning muscle and spatial coordination and accidents are going to happen now and then. You don't want everyone to be living in fear and on their nerves at every mealtime. That won't help anyone's digestion.
- If the child is sitting on a proper chair, when a little bigger, prop them up with a booster seat or cushions so that they're high enough to eat comfortably.

- Help smaller children to cut up their food, if needed.

And of course, you need to be demonstrating the table manners you eventually want them to learn. By about six, a child should be able to sit at the table, on a proper chair, wiggle-free, and have basic manners for around 20 minutes or so.

What are good table manners? In general, they include:

- To ask for items instead of reaching across others.
- To wait until everyone has been served before starting to eat, and to say grace or give thanks first if that's part of your family mealtime.
- To place your napkin on your lap.
- To keep your elbows off the table and closer to the body. No "flying" or knocking your neighbor during meals.
- To eat with your fork in the left hand and knife in the right hand.
- To chew with your mouth closed. And no talking with food in your mouth.
- To not groom yourself at the table, burp, fart, or otherwise disgust your dinner partners with your bodily functions.
- To engage in dinner conversation, which includes no rude or revolting stories that might put people off their food. Also to follow general conversational manners: not interrupt and not talk about anything stressful or potentially conflictual at this time. Keep those conversations for another setting.
- To chew slowly and enjoy the meal.
- To wait until people have finished their meals before leaving the table.
- To ask to be excused from the table when finished, or if you have to answer a call of nature.

Mealtimes can be enjoyable moments full of the pleasure of good food and good company. This can be a relaxed way to teach all kinds of manners to your children in a friendly, calm way. Mealtimes can be something the family looks forward to, as a time to reconnect and check in with each other.

By the time you need to take your children out in public or to someone's home, if you have been living a mannerly home life, as detailed above, you're sure to be getting some compliments on how well-behaved they are.

Noise Levels

Little children don't seem to have a volume control. Loud cries, roars, and even screaming reverberate whether they're happy or sad. But as they get a bit bigger, you can start teaching an awareness of noise levels.

This is part of respecting others, whether at home or out. Noise is stressful, drowns out whatever you're trying to say, and pollutes the atmosphere. Frankly, we could all do with less of it.

Places and times where noise is especially unwelcome are:

- Libraries, where people go to read and browse in peace.
- At work or school, where people need to concentrate.
- At special events like musical shows, plays, funerals, weddings, in church, at conferences, and talks.
- At night, when people are trying to sleep. Also in the evenings when everyone is wanting to relax and small babies sleep early. I think a polite guideline for loud or invasive noise of any sort is to keep it down between 7 p.m. and 8 a.m. at the minimum. Various municipalities will have different noise guidelines, but to be a good neighbor, it helps to put yourself in other people's shoes. For example, drilling or some other external racket

before 9 a.m. on a Sunday is more than a little frustrating to the weekly worker who was desperately hoping for a weekend sleep-in.
- In restaurants, where diners hope to have a modicum of peace while eating and would like to be able to hear themselves speak at their own table, at least.
- In places where, out of respect, noise is unwelcome, like graveyards, churches, museums, and similar.

Sometimes you might need to remind your kids about how loud they are, as often people don't have that awareness, especially children when they get excited. I have a dear friend who has no "inside" voice and talks so loudly that people across the room know all her private business whether they want to or not. Her parents never created this awareness for her, and it shows.

Basic Hygiene

You might not think this is a manners thing, but really it is. Hygiene is obviously necessary for health reasons, and not just our own but that of the people around us too. Being aware of how our lack of hygiene can impact others and taking steps to prevent it is also an example of good manners.

This is an area that school-going kids and teens often need a lot of reminding about. But it helps to explain the 'why' as well as the 'what', so that they don't think you're just being too nitpicky.

Someone who looks grubby, has mucky hair, dirty hands, clothes or face, smells bad, and everything else that goes with poor hygiene, is really off-putting. Socially, they're going to be avoided by others because being around them is unpleasant. This extends to how they live at home too. A messy house is one thing, but a deeply dirty house is a place I certainly don't want to visit. Instilling some pride in self and awareness of these issues in your child can start from quite early on. As they get bigger, teach them about germs and how they can spread.

Encourage them to use their senses.

- Does it smell bad? If so, what can we do to clean up or reduce the bad smell? Things like regular bathing, using deodorant, and cleaning out our bags, cars, and homes from time to time all contribute to better odors.
- Does it look bad? Messy, unbrushed hair, torn or dirty clothes, beaten up shoes, and the like, all contribute to a poor first or ongoing impression of the person who lives like that.
- Does it feel bad? Sticky hands, crumbs all over the floor, and grubby belongings feel unpleasant to the touch.

Some basic areas of hygiene include:

- Daily toothbrushing (twice a day) and keeping your breath fresh. Nobody wants to get close or talk to someone with halitosis breath.
- Daily bathing and use of deodorant or use of a body spray, especially when kids get into puberty. You may find that they also start to experiment with perfume or cologne. But a little of that is preferred rather than a lot, though, as it can be overpowering, and certainly in many schools and other public spaces, perfume is frowned upon or banned due to allergies.
- Wearing clean clothes.
- Brushing hair, cleaning fingernails, and covering any open wounds.
- Washing and sanitizing hands, and in these times, wearing a face mask.
- Coughing or sneezing into your elbow or a tissue and not your hands or the open air.

- Keeping your area tidy and clean. Putting dirty dishes in the dishwasher or sink and washing them. Wiping down kitchen counters with sanitizing solutions, and keeping bathrooms sanitized, too. There is obviously more to it than this, and if you involve your child in household chores from early on, they will grow to understand what's needed.

Good hygiene means that your presence is not physically offensive to others, and also that you're not causing a potential health risk to the greater community. It shows respect for others to practice it properly.

Tidying Up

Get into the habit of teaching a tidy-up-time routine to your kids from early on. Whether at home or at a playdate, once playtime is over, good manners means picking up and putting away your toys.

Your mess is your responsibility.

This thinking extends into all areas of life but starts with a child picking up their toys. How you do this is up to you. Some parents limit the number of toys that can be taken out at one time and have clever storage systems or shelves where pictures of each item show the child where it needs to go. Putting back some toys before taking others out is also a good idea.

At first, you will need to help small children, and you can make it more appealing by having races, singing songs, and so on. By the age of four, children should understand what tidy up means.

Older children can be expected to tidy up after themselves in their rooms, common living spaces, and also when a guest in other homes. If you have eaten dinner in someone's home, offer to help clean dishes. Some people will accept and others not, and it's perfectly fine to follow their wishes in each case.

When out and about, if you drop litter, pick it up. As part of a community drive, I often involve my kids in a general litter pick-up in the neighborhood, which also teaches them respect for the environment and helping others.

Finally, if your pet (or small child) messes up, it's also your responsibility to clean up.

Shopping

Basic shopping etiquette can be taught to preschoolers and older kids as part of your shopping outings.

Over and above the general "out and about" guidelines, when in a shop, you should:

- Walk on the left or right of the aisles, depending on your region's general direction of travel.
- Keep to one side and don't make it difficult for other people to move past you. That includes not bunching up in groups with friends to have a social catch-up and blocking the aisles for everyone else.
- Allow other shoppers time to browse the shelves in front of them. There is a horrible trend for impatient and selfish people to rush and hurry everyone who isn't them. Another bad habit is ducking in front of a person to grab what you want when they are browsing the shelf in front of them.
- Not touch or squeeze all the unwrapped, fresh produce or take items and then put them back in the wrong places. If you need to feel if an item is ripe, be gentle so as not to bruise the produce for the next person. It might sound a bit extreme, but personally, I think it's better to

just buy and ripen at home. And I always wipe off my fresh produce with a mild sanitizing solution before storing at home, because you know that many hands have probably touched it.

- Pick up anything you drop and put it back where it belongs. If it breaks (or is already broken), let a shop assistant know.
- At the checkout, put your items through, pay, and move on at a reasonable pace, but don't rush or be impatient with those in front of you who need time to put away their card or change and wallet before moving on. A few seconds of patience will not kill you, and in turn, others may be more patient when it's your turn.
- Always be friendly and polite to the cashiers. They have a tedious and exhausting job, and a smiling face helps lighten the load. I've heard some dreadful horror stories about how rude customers can be, often quoting "the customer is always right" to cover up their lack of courtesy. In the end, any amount of rudeness is totally unnecessary and just downright bad behavior; you can easily request whatever it is you need politely.
- Once you've unloaded your shopping cart, take it back to the corral at the shop entrance.

All of these habits show respect for the needs and time of other shoppers as well as the shop staff, who definitely notice and appreciate it when you don't make their day any harder.

Using the Phone

Nothing annoys me more than a caller ringing me up and disrespecting me by:

- Not greeting me politely.
- Not identifying themselves.

- Not stating why they're calling.

Spam and telemarketing callers are insidious with this invasive approach, although lately I screen all of those calls anyway. My time is precious, and if I want to buy something, I'll go online to look for it.

Answering any phone requires you to greet the caller and say something polite, which might be along the lines of "How may I help you?" in the most formal setting or much more casual at home.

Teaching small kids to talk on the phone can be done with the help of friends or family members who are patient and understanding. Little kids may not know when they're expected to speak or reply and might need help with this. In my house, to keep things simple and to make sure we get the messages we need to get, we have a house rule that if you don't know how to answer a phone, or are less than a meter high, you shouldn't be doing it.

Calling someone and getting their barely verbal two-year-old who drops the phone, turns it off, or cannot call a parent can be frustrating, especially when it's an important call.

Telephone conversations follow the general conversational guidelines already discussed, but there's no harm in politely cutting an unwanted call short, or simply not answering them. There are plenty of apps that help you identify who is calling so that you can avoid speaking to anyone you wish.

The problem with phones is that the caller has no idea if you're in the middle of dinner, in the bathroom, napping, in an important meeting, or otherwise engaged. It helps to turn your phone off or mute the ringer at these times. If you set and protect your boundaries, then it saves you annoyance and you're not tempted to take it out on a person who could be oblivious to what they were interrupting.

Now that mobiles are ubiquitous, everybody is "always on". No place is really free from the invasiveness of these devices, with the possible exception of theaters, if you're lucky. Of course, they are really handy, but many people haven't thought about how their use affects others.

In general, when using a cell phone:

- Take calls outside or away from any social gatherings where you can't be overheard or disrupt others. Keep your voice down; the people at the next table truly are not interested in your life.
- Keep your ringer off in libraries, music events, plays, talks, and any place where quiet is expected.
- Turn your device off or leave it stowed away when at dinner or in the middle of a conversation or meeting. I once had a date play a game on his phone at a really nice restaurant. He ignored me, the service staff, and everyone else. Needless to say, that was his last date with me.
- Don't take calls when you're in the bathroom. The caller can generally hear what you're doing, especially the flush.

Mobile devices are useful tools and don't need to be blamed for all of society's ills as long as we learn how to use them with consideration.

Emails and Messages

Again, with our emails and messages on our mobile devices, more often than not we can fall into the "always on" trap.

Management of your messages is a life skill you can teach your children as they grow older.

- Have a set time of day when you check and reply to emails and messages so that the rest of your time isn't

- gobbled up with continual messaging. This frees you up to focus on other constructive activities in between.
- Don't leave messages without a reply for longer than 24 hours if you can help it, but don't get into the habit of instantly replying to everything, either, unless you want your life to be ruled by it. Of course, urgent messages can be responded to as needed.
- If you send an important email or message, it can be a good idea to follow up with a phone call to ensure the person has seen it, knows why it's important, and will attend to it in the required time frames. But consider that person's boundaries too; some people object to receiving a phone call about the same thing you sent a message about.
- Be careful of your tone in a written message. Often emails and messages can come across much harsher than intended because they don't have the body language or facial expressions that help to convey the intention. If you're upset, put off mailing or messaging until you feel more balanced, and don't hit 'send' until you feel calmer and have read through the text a few times.

Social Media

This can be a difficult one for kids to take on board because social media is such an integral part of their lives. But they to need to be aware that anything put on a public forum, or even in a closed group of friends, is open to public censure. People will judge you based on what you are posting. Not only that, but once it's in the public domain, it will exist forever, whether you want it to or not.

It has taken some time for everyone to understand that these platforms are also legally admissible, and so great care must be taken before posting anything. In general don't:

- Post anything that is very personal, profane, rude, abusive, pornographic, illegal, racist, sexist, or otherwise bigoted or threatening to others. People have been slapped with civil and criminal lawsuits over stuff like this, and once posted, the comments become part of a permanent record, even if you delete them later.
- Tag anyone in photographs or comments without their consent. Most apps and platforms let users limit what others can tag them in, and you can set yours up in the same way to avoid this issue.
- Lose awareness of who can see what you post. Many employers, student boards, schools, and others will check your social media, and if they can see pictures of all your party nights, comments about how you hate your current teacher or job, or other personal things, that may affect you negatively.

Online trolls and bullies abound, and luckily you have the law on your side if people are threatening you in any way. Teach your children that they don't need to retaliate online. Take screenshots and identify the person before going to the authorities if the behavior is disturbing or continuous. You also have the ability to electronically block anyone who is threatening or offensive.

Respecting Your Elders and Authority Figures

It's a complex concept for children, but as they mature they can be taught that older doesn't necessarily mean wiser. Everyone is on their own path of learning, maturity, and consciousness. Grownups also make mistakes and make bad choices.

To your child, adults– or anyone older than them—may be seen as a figure of authority and also safety when, in fact, they might not be. It's a good idea to teach kids that just because someone is older than you doesn't mean they automatically deserve respect or obedience. But it also doesn't mean that they should be disrespected. Teach children to judge for themselves.

Remind them that they can ask for help from another source if an authority figure or older person is:

- Asking them to do something wrong or harmful to themselves or others.
- Asking them to keep a secret.
- Making them feel scared, unhappy, or unsettled.
- Behaving badly. For example, shouting, hurting, banging, not being in control of themselves, and so on.

However, in general, if a person is not doing any of the above, then a certain amount of respect should be shown. This can include:

- Asking for advice from someone who has more life experience or knowledge.
- Being friendly and polite and using all your regular good manners.
- Assisting elderly people who are clearly struggling with a task and letting them have your seat if seating is limited.
- Cooperating with reasonable requests of authority figures like policemen, traffic officers, and teachers.

Often, older people may get left out or forgotten in the day-to-day functions of life, so if you have elderly people in the family or neighborhood, take the time to check in with them, chat with them, and offer assistance if needed. Ask about their lives and listen. There's a lot we can learn from the past, even if in the end we're all somewhat flawed humans.

Respecting Diversity

What constitutes good manners may vary from place to place, and even from family to family. These days, we have many diverse cultures living alongside each other as well. The best approach is to use your normal good manners and simply to ask if you're unsure.

The internet is also a great source of information about different religions, cultures, and ways of living. Doing a little research into what is considered good manners or offensive before visiting a foreign country or going into the home of people with different cultural backgrounds will never be time wasted. For example, pointing with your hand or foot in many eastern countries is highly offensive. In Thailand, if you accidentally stand on paper money (which has the face of their king on it) you could even go to jail.

Teaching kids to respect all forms of diversity is important if they're to get along in a very diverse world. Discrimination is heavily frowned upon and doesn't win anyone any awards. In fact, openly biased, discriminatory words and deeds can land you in some pretty hot water socially and legally and can affect everything from your lifestyle to your livelihood. It's way past time to let go of whatever we think we know about people who are different from us and start opening up to rehumanizing and respecting all of our fellow beings on this planet.

Anything that denigrates and breaks down a person based on an innate characteristic that they're born with is usually based on fear, over-inflated egos, insecurity, past history (which often dehumanized people for economic reasons), and a failure to question the status quo or poor behavior of previous generations.

A respect for diversity, like most good manners, will be best learned by the example you yourself set.

- Examine your own biases and the stereotypes you may believe with regard to anyone who is different from you. Look for counterevidence and examples of people who disprove any existing biases you may have. Ask yourself lots of questions, the main one being, "What is my root belief about [x]?" And then, "Why do I think this?" Keep digging down until you understand and can see where unhelpful judgments may have originated. This by itself can often turn the whole erroneous idea on its head.
- Watch the language and stories you use around your children and be mindful of your own biases creeping out in your words and deeds.
- Don't limit your kids to gender-appropriate toys. Let them choose what they want to play with. All play develops various abilities and is therefore useful. For example, doll play encourages caring and empathy, car play develops spatial skills. Kids need all these skills, regardless of gender.
- Make sure that everyone helps with chores; Dad and Mom, brothers and sisters.
- Encourage empathy, kindness, and compassion.
- Encourage curiosity and answer any questions about differences as openly and honestly as possible.
- Expose your children to the stories, movies, and ways of life of a range of different types of people. Be open to discussing these and answering questions.

An open, enquiring mind and the ability to be curious and compassionate rather than fearful and aggressive towards anyone different from us is one of the most valuable abilities you can teach your children.

4

Raising a Responsible Kid

Watching my children start taking responsibility for chores, for themselves and their own lives always gives me a little thrill of happiness. It may be something small, like they feed the dog or take out the trash without being asked, but it means you have leveled up. It also means that they have taken a big step to becoming more self-sufficient and able to survive out there in the world without you.

These little signs of responsibility that come from the child's own sense of investment in their home and the other people and animals in it, or to their own schoolwork, or wherever it occurs are signs that an important lesson has been internalized. Once that happens, it's fairly easy to extend that to other areas of life.

Building a sense of responsibility and personal investment in your children doesn't happen overnight. It grows out of self-awareness, empathy, and also awareness of what it takes to live in this world. As they show they are able, by giving them increased responsibility, you empower them, build their self-confidence, and allow them to learn vital skill sets they will need later on in life.

A sense of responsibility is an important personal characteristic that you definitely want your kids to have. A responsible person will display healthy behaviors like owning their mistakes and taking steps to fix them. They know what they are accountable for, and also what they're not. They will look around them at the world and take an interest and an active role in improving what they can because they know that we are all part of a cohesive, mutually linked system. They don't wait for life to happen to them, they decide what they need to do and then do it. Responsibility doesn't mean taking on all the world's burdens, but it does mean being actively involved in doing what falls within your sphere of influence.

Many people over-parent and feel they need to show their care and love by doing everything for their kids. This could be a reaction to their own past childhood neglect when they were kids, or based on fear for their children. Unfortunately, by limiting your child's chances to do things for themselves and for other people, you may inadvertently be limiting your child in life. This diminishes a child's confidence and belief that they can do things themselves and puts the responsibility always elsewhere. Chipping away at a child's confidence in their own abilities can foster a weak, victim mentality, or a person who lacks the belief in self that they need to get on and get things done.

Building Responsible Minds

There are several ways you can lay the foundation for a child to eventually become an empowered and responsible person.

Let Them do it Themselves

Although it can be painful to watch your little one struggle to peel a banana, tie their laces, get dressed, and so on, it's important to let them try. Give them the space to attempt the thing they want to do. If they're getting frustrated or they ask for help, then step in and demonstrate how and see if they want to try again for themselves. Or give them just enough help so that they can complete the task themselves. For example, half peeling the banana, and letting them do the rest.

"Me do it!" was an everyday sentence I heard with all my babies, and I respected their determination to try. Now they're all growing up confidently, and they're not afraid to try new things, or hard things, on their own.

Clean Up Your Own Messes

From early on, teach responsibility by showing your kids that they have to take responsibility for any mess—literal or other—that they make. This means letting them clean up their own spills, wash the crayon scribble off the wall, and put away their toys. It may not be a perfect job, and you can always rectify that when they aren't around to see. You want them to make the connection early on that if they do a thing, they need to fix whatever happens next, if necessary.

This also means letting them face the music if they forget homework, don't complete assignments, leave school projects to the last minute, forget their lunch, or whatever it is they were required to do for their day ahead. I've been called hard for not rushing to their rescue, but it didn't take long for them to internalize that they had to be responsible and that if they weren't, they would face the consequences. It also meant less stress for me, as I wasn't running around after them all the time. It might sound tough, but it's a kind of tough love, and it can be achieved with kindness and compassion. You can empathize with their plight but not take it on as your own. For example, with an older, school-going child, "Yes, I understand it's 8 p.m. and you haven't learned your poem for class tomorrow, but you had all afternoon to do it. You chose to play computer games instead, didn't you? That's not my problem, that's yours to handle. You'll need to talk to your teacher and see what she says."

It's a good idea to confirm the facts of a situation too. You don't want to overlook something along the lines of a learning challenge, or some other real issue your child does need your help with. But these little incidents are not generally dangerous or harmful. If you know your child is able to do the things they have to do, that they have the resources and yet choose not to do so in good time, it's not bad parenting to let them experience the consequences. This is a natural learning curve that will teach them a valuable life lesson if you just let the situation to come to its natural conclusion.

Obviously, small kids need more help, but from about five or six, most kids can be allowed to take over packing their bags, making their own lunches the night before, and so on. Some children will need reminding from time to time, and it doesn't hurt to keep an eye on things. But always remind, step away, and then let them fix the thing they forgot.

Let Them Help

From early on, you can involve your child in daily tasks. Toddlers love washing up, sweeping, packing, unpacking, counting, fetching, and carrying. At this age, it's a novelty and fun for them. As they get older, they may be less enthusiastic, but you can still engage them in daily activities that contribute to the family unit.

Ask Them What They Think is Needed

Preschoolers and more verbal kids can be involved on an intellectual level with daily family life. Share with them what everyone is doing, and even show them how it's done. Let them know what it takes to run a home in an open, friendly fashion. Kids may not notice this stuff until it's pointed out to them. Honestly, shopping, cleaning and the like probably isn't that interesting for them. But you can engage their interest by talking about it and explaining how one day they will be doing all of this stuff for themselves in their own homes. You can involve them and make it more engaging with a little creativity. For example, giving your school-age child a little money and letting them choose healthy ingredients for lunch for everyone at the shop.

Once they have an idea of what's going on around them, ask them what part of it they would like to help with. If they choose their own chores, they will be way more invested in doing them.

Give and Encourage Structure

While it takes all types to make a world, and not everyone enjoys routine and structure, it's generally better for small kids when their little world follows some sort of schedule. It becomes a safe, known series of events, which helps growing children let go of uncertainty and any fear around that. It creates a framework within which they have more freedom to relax and enjoy themselves. It also makes sure that essentials like food, hydration, sleep, play, learning, and other self-care don't get overlooked. These more structured individuals will consistently have their basic needs met, which will contribute to better health and resilience.

Using structure for and with your children helps demonstrate to them how this works. It also teaches them these skills so that they can lead more balanced lives and manage their time and responsibilities effectively.

Use Repair Rather than Retribution

It's tempting when you feel angry to lash out, lose your cool, and punish your child for some wrongdoing. This doesn't help either of you feel any better, and certainly doesn't teach what you were hoping. Pain, harsh words, and other punishments generally only work in the short term and teach that this punishing behavior is okay. This is how abusive cycles continue throughout generations in families.

A more lasting, constructive way both to achieve the desired behavior from your child and to set the foundation for responsibility is to let the fix be the consequence. That might mean an apology and also an action to make amends. Involve your child in deciding what the best action might be. It could be performing a service to directly repair the problem caused or donating time and effort to a charity or someone else in need. When apologizing, the act offered to make amends must be open to negotiation, as the person harmed by the bad behavior might have their own ideas about what will make this problem better for them.

Blame vs. Solution-Based Thinking

When you're stuck in a fault-finding mentality and looking for someone to blame for a problem, that sets the scene for isolation, defensiveness, and resentment. It can also result in children hiding stuff because they don't want to take the blame, as it's so unpleasant. That's how lies can start becoming a problem, too.

We have a basic rule in our home: admit your mistakes. Take responsibility for what you did or did not do, and then everyone will pull together to help. You might still be in some trouble, but the focus will be on helping you to fix the problem and avoid it happening again. This is a far more constructive approach that encourages kids to own up to their share of what went wrong. It also teaches problem-solving and leaves the child feeling more motivated to do better in the future.

Let Them Work for Pay

Clearly linking a money value to various household chores, or letting your child earn by doing small, neighborhood chores for others, is a great way to incentivize getting things done. For older children, it gives them some freedom to purchase things they want, and grants a sense of responsibility both around the paying tasks and with managing the money they earn.

While I prefer using praise and recognition or mutual reciprocity, rewards like food treats, special time or events, and money that they can use for these things, too, all form very powerful rewards that reinforce more of that helpful behavior down the line.

Household Chores

One of the best ways to start teaching responsibility is with everyday life in the home. The chores and responsibilities that you have to do to run a household or to care for loved ones and pets are all perfect opportunities to foster a sense of responsibility in your children.

Practical Exercise: Sharing the Load

As a family, sit down and brainstorm all the things that need to be done daily, weekly, monthly, and annually.

- How big is each task? Are there sub-steps to the larger ones? Rate them big, medium, or small.
- How complicated is each task? Rate them hard, average, or easy.
- Are there any tasks that need to be done by specific people, and why?
- Let everyone look at the remaining tasks and negotiate who will do what.
- Assign tasks and workload by age and ability, making sure that no one person is overloaded or underloaded.
- You can write (or draw) these up on a chore list or board as a visual reminder for everyone.

- You can link incentives like a star chart, pocket money, special treats or outings, or whatever is valuable to each child to help the process along.

As a family, you all create the necessity for certain tasks, like laundry, cleaning, and eating. Therefore, you should all contribute to the related activities as part of contributing to the group and its success.

Age-Appropriate Chores

Under three years old: These babies can be given a play broom and duster or be allowed to play in a basin of soapy water with their own food dishes after meals. Always watch a small child closely where even a small amount of water is involved, as drownings can happen even in a few centimeters of liquid. At this age, it's just play, and no real results can possibly be expected.

From three to five years old: Once a child is walking and talking, they can be involved in simple chores like carrying safe items and laying them on the dinner table, sweeping or vacuuming, standing on a booster step to help wash dishes, brushing pets, walking pets with help, dusting, and picking up toys. They can also fetch and carry small, safe items. Again, at this stage the aim is to make it more of a fun group activity, and you cannot expect any sort of perfection. You're just laying the groundwork for later and getting them used to being involved and helping out.

From six to ten years old: By now, your child's cognitive and physical abilities should be fairly reliable and advanced. They can help with things like packing and unpacking a dishwasher, making their own school lunches and packing schoolbooks, loading the washing machine and dryer, putting away toys, picking up after a pet, taking out trash, wiping kitchen counters, setting and clearing the table, walking the dog with help, grooming, cleaning, and feeding pets, putting away their own clothes, and helping fold laundry.

From 11 to 15 years old: They can continue with the earlier chores and also be expected to manage their own schoolwork with fewer reminders, watch younger siblings during the day, make simple meals, and perform more complex tasks.

From 15 years upwards: These teens and young adults can start helping with the shopping, watching younger siblings for short periods during the day or night, and be counted on to complete agreed upon chores with little or no need for reminding or guidance. They can be expected to fully care for a pet, including solo walks and vet visits.

Once they have their driver's licenses, they can even drive their siblings to events, do bulk grocery shops, or run other errands for you. By now they're nearly considered adults but will still need some oversight, depending on their level of competence and responsibility.

5

Manners Challenges

Sometimes we only realize we're sitting with a real problem when our children have reached the age at which they should know the difference between good manners and bad, and yet they're showing no signs of doing the right things or getting it right only some of the time.

You can find yourself in this position for a whole range of reasons, but as you don't have a time machine, unfortunately, to go back to the beginning, you'll have to deal with what's in front of you. The teen years can be especially challenging. Even if your child was doing well up until this point, they can suddenly switch into a rude and unpleasant person you barely know at the drop of a hat.

Helping Children Improve Manners

When faced with problematic behavior, a few things will go through your mind. First will be your own annoyance and reactive state. We've already spoken about how to avoid this kind of reaction, and we know that our anger and frustration will only complicate the situation. Take a deep breath, count, walk away, whatever it takes to stop yourself from exploding, and then deal with the situation when you're calmer.

First off, if you did not manage to contain your knee-jerk reaction, demonstrate good manners by apologizing for what you did wrong or handled badly. Clear the air. A defensive, fearful, or angry child will definitely not be open to learning anything from you, so that's the first bridge to cross.

When everyone has had a chance to calm down, have a quiet discussion. Include everyone who was involved if you can. Talk about what's going on in everyone's day or life. Perhaps your kid has had a rough day at school or is feeling anxious or a bit blue. Feel it out a little before you dive in with solutions and reprimands.

Once that's done, talk about what's okay and not okay and why. Remind everyone about the ground rules and what they look like in real life. Let them do a lot of the talking and use questions to prompt them. If you open the discussion with, "Do you know what didn't work here?" or "Can you tell me what you think just went wrong?", that will put the ball in their court and enable them to release emotions by expressing their thoughts and feelings.

Throughout these experiences, always remember that you are the adult with years of experience and maturity. So, your behavior has to be better than theirs. You need to show them how it's done, how to solve their problems, and how to handle conflict effectively. If you're losing your cool, how can you expect them to do any better? You need to be the safe space, safety net, and wise mentor all rolled into one.

We often expect children and teens to think as we do, but if you think back to your own childhood, you probably didn't have it all together either. Kids can do or say utterly illogical, short-sighted things. Most likely, they won't yet have any idea of what it's like in the real world, or what they'll need to be and do to survive. They can only express themselves from their own point of understanding, and they may not have given anything that much thought yet. It can leave you shaking your head in wonderment. But, you're applying mature adult logic to someone who is likely hormonal, emotional, often quite self-absorbed, and who may express their intense feelings in some very random ways.

As they grow, it's normal for them to test you to see where the boundaries are and push your hot buttons on purpose. I see this, in part, as them checking in to see if they're still loved and valued. Teens need reassurance as they navigate tricky times with their bodies, their friends, schools, and a pretty scary, confusing world. It's common for them to take out their tensions where they feel safe: with you. When they act up and you're able to remain calm, loving, and constructive, this pours soothing water on the flames rather than oil. If you lose your temper, you've lost the plot and won't be able to parent like you need to.

If you do have to apply disciplinary consequences, do so consistently. If bad behavior is deliberate and ongoing, apply the rules as calmly as you can. You can give a final warning, but if the bad behavior continues, you may need to give a time out or withdraw privileges and certain freedoms that they enjoy. You can also go the whole making amends, fixing your own mess, and the reparation route we spoke about before.

Sometimes a normally polite kid may occasionally lash out. Be tolerant. They could well be on another mental planet, self-absorbed, or emotional about something unrelated to you and unaware of how badly they're behaving. Perhaps you caught them at a bad time; we all have those. Allow them to calm down, and remind them that that kind of behavior is not okay. Give them a chance to apologize. I often just say, "Is that a good way to behave?" That still shows them that what they are doing is wrong and lets them reflect. Within minutes, I will have received a heartfelt apology.

Another lament I hear many parents making is the issue of chores and teens. Suddenly your kid doesn't want to pull their weight or procrastinates with everything until the very last minute. I've found that it's definitely best to keep this stuff as matter-of-fact and as non-confrontational as you can. Give a warning, and then act on the stated consequence. But do it in a way that mimics real-world consequences and that also matches the misdemeanor. For example, if they leave dirty clothes all over their room, simply do not pick them up and wash them. Let them pile up. Offer your teen a demonstration of how the washing machine works, and let them wash their own when they eventually run out. Dirty cups and plates can pile up, too. Just close their bedroom door or ban them from using the good stuff and only allow them paper cups and plates so their hoarding doesn't interfere with the rest of the family's need for crockery. I have known some parents to plant peppercorns or pawpaw seeds in their kid's room and pretend it was rat droppings. A bit of a subterfuge, but it appeared to work. Ultimately, your child will get through this messy stage and start taking more pride in their surroundings again. And if not, this will be their life problem, as hopefully they won't be living with you forever.

Another natural consequence of you having to do their chores is that when they need you to take them somewhere or do something for them, you can point out that all your spare time was used doing their chores so you can't help them. There is also the removal of devices or online privileges. I've been known to turn off or change the wifi password from time to time when I needed to make a point. What also worked well for us was letting our teen "buy" online and gaming time with the chores and tasks that had to be completed first.

Teens are not that great at planning for the future or stopping when they're in the middle of enjoying an activity to go do a chore. So reminders in the form of visual lists and verbal reminders may help. Don't make it into a battle; just play to your own strengths, stay in control of your reactions, and wait them out.

Always say thank you for the good stuff they do. Show your appreciation and tell them you are proud of whatever they are getting right. Be specific. Try to catch them at the time of the good deeds. Praise their good behavior to others, too, where they can hear you.

The things kids do and the choices they make won't always make sense. Just be a loving parent anyway and be patient while they grow up and learn better with your help.

Coming Late to the Manners Game

If you're in charge of a school-going kid or a teenager who has never been taught manners before now, you need a slightly different approach. Older kids are able to argue you under the table, and they will debate with you, ignore you, or worse.

To start late means you will need to:

- Get their respect by behaving well, no matter how badly they behave.
- Be calm and patient.
- Be clear and firm when required. If you waver and give in because it feels too hard or you're too busy, you're not communicating a consistent message. What you're doing is giving in, and that means they quickly learn they can push you hard enough to get their own way and that it works—a bad lesson for everyone.

- Don't assume the worst or jump to conclusions; always try to get all the facts of a situation first by asking lots of questions.
- Make an effort to understand their world, point of view, and challenges.
- Explain the reasons for the behavior you want.
- Discuss expectations on both sides and agree on what's possible for both of you, where you might need to compromise, and what you're prepared to do.
- Share what's negotiable and what's not, as well as the consequences of ongoing bad behavior.
- Build a relationship outside of the manners issue. Share interests, do things together, and try to find common ground and shared passions.

You won't achieve perfection, but you can work towards a more civil child if you persist for long enough.

How Not to Raise a Liar

A certain amount of "untruth" can be expected from most kids. In fact, paradoxically, the ability to lie can be beneficial. On the spectrum of truth and dishonesty, you'll find that many socially required behaviors require some holding back of the entire truth. It's those brutally honest people who explain away their harsh words with "I'm only telling the truth" that nobody tends to like very much. What these ruthless truthsayers believe to be true is coupled with a lack of kindness, awareness, and compassion, and harms more often than it helps. For example, while everyone knows that someone has a big nose (as does the person with the nose, undoubtedly), do they need to be told about it by some other "well-meaning" person all the time? The intention needs questioning. What are you trying to achieve with your truth? Does the other person not know already? How will this knowledge help them, and is it even true? Or is it just true for you?

What the truth is, is also open to interpretation based on each person's unique outlook on life and grasp of reality. Seldom do we have all the real facts of any situation. What we have, generally, are assumptions, beliefs, interpretations, and imagination. This cognitive filter, or bias, is apparent when a crowd of people are called upon to report an accident or event they have witnessed. Each person will have a different version of the scene. They are not intentionally lying, but their viewpoints may not be 100% correct, either.

White lies, flights of imagination, not saying everything that's on your mind, or holding back certain facts to protect the listener are all acceptable forms of lying in our society. Most of us do it all the time. "No, I'm busy and can't make it," you say to that invite when in fact you're planning to take that day to watch your favorite TV series. "I'm fine," you say to that stranger, when in fact you're not, but there's no point in sharing your complex life situation with someone who is being invasive of your privacy and can't help you anyway. Similarly, you don't generally blurt out all the bad things a person did at their funeral; it's just not appropriate at that time. "Pleased to meet you," you say to that new work colleague, when in fact you're wishing you were on a yacht in the Mediterranean, and feel zero pleasure at meeting yet another person at your workplace. "Father Christmas is coming," you tell your small children, along with many other untrue fantasies about the tooth fairy, Easter bunny, and more.

I am sure most people can recall dozens of times they have done this kind of thing. There will be some who insist on 100% honesty, and if you're able to do that without disclosing all your private details or upsetting others and have a sound, objective grasp of reality (are you sure about that?), then well done. The more honest and authentic you can be with yourself and with the world in general, the better. Just so long as you can do it kindly and mindfully as well.

So, we have to teach our children not only what to say but also when it's appropriate. We also need to teach them what not to say, and what falls within an acceptable range of truth versus untruth.

Kids start lying from about three years old. Between four and six, they often tell whoppers that are patently untrue, but these could be more just their imagination at play. Little kids often give themselves away with facial expressions and voices when they are trying on an obvious lie. Children lie because they:

- Are experimenting. This type of lie should be allowed to some degree, as it shows creativity and learning. If your child tells you a long story about a magic owl who brought her a gift, you can hear her out. You know she is merely practicing her creativity and exercising her imaginary world.
- Want extra attention. In this case, you can withdraw attention for the lying behavior and see where else you can give positive reinforcement for behavior you want.
- Want to avoid trouble. This means that perhaps there is too much of a blame or punishment culture being applied. You need to reduce the fear and increase the love and constructive solutions. Step back and get solution-focused. Discuss why truth is important. Without it, we can't fix problems or learn what we need to do.
- Want to get something. This type of lie should be called out and dealt with. Whatever they wanted cannot be given in reward for a lie. This will have to be explained, and you can point out that if you're caught being devious, you lose people's trust, and why it's more important to keep this trust than get a temporary benefit. It helps if all the adults in the house are communicating fully around this stuff to avoid a child playing one off against the other. Look at putting a

rewards system in place that allows them to get what they want with good behavior rather than lies.
- Want to avoid hurting another person's feelings. In this case, evaluate the situation. What was the intention, and what was the result? Was it helpful or harmful?

Of course, we don't want our kids to get into the habit of harmful or unhelpful untruths. So how do we go about making sure that doesn't happen?

- Discuss the basics of what a lie is and what truth is. Explain that honesty will attract trust, loyalty, and respect, and that it's brave and feels good when you don't live with lies to yourself or others. Let them ask lots of questions and give examples of what kinds of lies are not acceptable and what the consequences will be if they're caught in this kind of lie.
- Manage your reactions to lies. Make it clear that honesty, no matter what has happened, will get a more favorable and supportive response than a lie will.
- Don't create situations that lead to lies. Confronting a child with questions around an accident or problem can push them into a lie out of fear and self-defense. Rather, just note what you have observed and then look at solutions together. For example, your child is supposed to feed the cat and you know he hasn't done it. Rather than saying, "Did you forget to feed the cat?" try "I see that the cat hasn't been fed, let's get that done."
- Praise them when they do own up to mistakes and problems. You can still apply some sort of consequence, like apologizing, fixing the problem, and so on, but you can do it more kindly.
- When a young child tells a tall tale, you can joke about it or simply listen and ask a few questions. For example, they say, "My dolly broke the cup." You can respond

- with, "Oh wow, that's interesting. I wonder why she did that?" You can keep this line of questions going until the truth emerges.
- If your kids make untruthful stories, simply listen to it as what it is–a make-believe story. You can even say, "That's a wonderful story. We could make that into a book." Encourage them to even write their ideas in a book and illustrate it. Who knows? You may have a budding writer, artist, or film producer on your hands.
- Avoid labeling your child as a liar. Rather, keep things constructive in the ways mentioned above.
- You can make a point of observing that you know when they aren't telling the truth. A sneaky way to do this is to link an observed tic or automatic behavior you have "noticed" they do when they lie. I told my son once that whenever he lied, I knew because he would not blink. Then when he was lying, he would make a point of blinking a lot. It was a dead giveaway. In effect, I created my own "tell sign", which, you may notice, was originally a lie I told to create awareness.
- Make a point of telling them when you know they aren't being completely honest but do so with all of the above in mind.

As you can see, it's a bit of a tricky path to navigate. As always, authenticity and honesty start with you. If you demonstrate the behavior you want, you are way more likely to get it from your child.

Bullies

About 50% of adults say they have been the victim of bullying, and yet less than 1% say they have ever bullied anybody. Clearly a lack of awareness is part of the problem.

Teaching your children about kindness, empathy, and boundaries from early on will give them the tools to deal with bullying behavior and also reduce the chances of they themselves becoming a bully. To not raise a bully, it starts with being aware of where your actions may be causing other people pain.

Bullying can be unintentional or a result of immaturity. It can be due to inner turmoil, isolation, or lack of social skills, and that can be remedied with helping the bully to grow insight and awareness. If we don't deal with it, it can become more serious. Bullying can become a way of life, and a way for them to get their own way, so any sign of it in our own families must be dealt with quickly.

Research shows that some people's brains light up in the pleasure center regions when they bully others. Sometimes we can literally see that a person is enjoying hurting others. This sociopathic behavior is a huge red flag. In cases like this, external help is needed to either help heal and socialize the perpetrator or to remove their ability to harm others.

But even if a child isn't a psychopath-in-training, any kind of consistently bad behavior towards others is a worrying habit that needs to be addressed. We should ask ourselves some tough questions: Are we guilty of such behavior? Might we need help with this? If we see it in our loved ones, we also should stop, assess, and take steps to lessen the harm.

When people end up feeling bad, demotivated, drained, and depressed; when the words used are toxic, critical, and destructive; when acts are harmful, hurtful, or abusive; or when choices have little concern with or for others, we call it bullying. It can even lead to physical or sexual assault if left unchecked. The victims of bullying get worn down, torn down emotionally, and fear, distrust, and dislike grow. The emotional and mental damage caused by bullying can lead to depression and even suicide in its victims.

You may have bully-proofed your own family and home. But even if everyone you know are loving, kind, aware, and empathic individuals, at some point there will come a time when your child is exposed to bullying in one form or another, and you might not be there to protect them. As they grow, learning these skills is vital for them to be able to survive in a sometimes harsh world.

To help your child deal with bullies:

- Teach them about boundaries and what is okay or not okay.
- Teach them how to set and reinforce boundaries, as we dealt with in an earlier chapter.
- Be clear on what bullying is:

  – Calling someone bad names or gossiping and spreading rumors about them.
  – Telling lies about others.
  – Physically hurting: hitting, punching, kicking, pinching, and so on.
  – Taking your stuff without your permission/stealing from you.
  – Damaging your belongings.
  – Socially isolating someone: like not including them in games, teams, or activities.
  – Threatening someone or intimidating them.

- When it's a stranger they don't need to see or hear from again, show them how to create space and distance between themselves and the bad behavior and how to ask for help if it's needed. Often our desire to "teach bullies a lesson" can backfire, and so showing kids how to respond rather than react, and always behave better than the bad guys, is an invaluable tool here.

- If a person they know and see a lot of is being a bully, like a classmate, teacher, cousin, or sibling, you may need to step in and help. When kids are first learning to set boundaries and protect themselves, they won't have the confidence or abilities to deal with a full-on assault from others. You can demonstrate how it's done and also let them know you're always there if they need you for protection. As they get older, just supporting them while they maintain their boundaries is usually enough. The key skills for dealing with bullies include:

– Not taking it personally. More often than not a bully is, themselves, experiencing inner pain and suffering. You can understand this and still not tolerate or condone the bad behavior.
– Being a nice human being. Sometimes showing a little kindness can defuse a bad situation. If that doesn't work, you can fall back on the next steps.
– Slowing the pace of your responses, if you need to make any at all. This will help you stay calm.
– Reward the good behavior and ignore or avoid the bad behavior.
– Stepping away from and avoiding the danger.
– Asking for help if things get out of hand.
– Think of ways of dealing with the touch points, where bullies are likely to prey on them. For example, on public transport or a school bus, your child can sit nearer to the driver. At school, they can sit nearer to the teacher's desk or with a group of supportive friends. They can avoid the places they know a bully hangs out, and possibly change their routes and timings to do so. Staying in a group of people also helps.

- Watch out for signs that your child is being bullied. They may be too embarrassed or frightened to ask for help.

Always look for out-of-the-ordinary changes in your child's behavior. Sudden, unexplained changes are always a sign of a problem. Children may withdraw, go quiet, start avoiding places or activities they used to enjoy, or become anxious, irritable, and moody. Unexplained bruises, missing or damaged property, and torn clothing are all signs. Changes in eating habits or school attendance or a sudden drop in grades can also indicate a problem. Frequent headaches and stomach aches or other ailments can be a result of stress, too.

- Some children are more vulnerable to bullying. School-going and teen years are very much an eat-or-be-eaten hotbed of social learning. Social pecking orders are harsh, and children can easily become isolated if they're a bit different from the average. This can mean a smart, creative kid, or one who is diverse due to culture, ability, race, religion, and even sexual orientation can easily become a target for other kids. You can't force all the other kids to behave well, but you can equip your child with the resilience and skills to withstand these times. Lots of family love and support, encouraging a few good friends, and continual work on self-awareness and self-worth will all help them through the more vulnerable years.
- Encourage your children to support anybody they see being bullied and to report what they see to an adult.

In today's online world, cyberbullying is a real issue, too. We see it in the crazy comment threads and trolling remarks all the time. Children can be especially sensitive and vulnerable to cyberbullying. It's probably a good idea to have this discussion with them when they are given access to their first online devices.

- Keep track of who has access to your child. Until they're old enough to deal with strangers, they shouldn't be

allowed unattended in chat rooms, online games, and the like. There are online predators who will pick on, or even worse, groom your child for future online or in-person abuse of all kinds. There are many nanny apps you can get to help you control this and limit what sites and people your child can access.
- If language is negative, toxic, and makes you feel "less than" or fearful, you are being bullied. If anyone sends threatening or horrible messages to your child, they can be reported to the police.
- Create an awareness around the fallout of online rudeness. It breaks people down. Not just the victim, but all the people who read it. It creates conflict, anger, and can push a person into depression or worse. Discuss examples of what is appropriate and what is not with your children.
- Being online allows people a certain sense of anonymity and distance. This means they tend to behave much worse than they would face to face. There is no excuse for ugly words and deeds. Discuss this with your kids and cover the following points:

– Reply with extra niceness to rudeness, if you have to reply at all. That way, you feel good and they feel stupid.
– Don't engage with random, mean strangers. Delete their comments or block them. Don't even reply once, as this feeds their bad habit. Any emotional response is giving them positive feedback.
– People can be ignorant or unkind, but you don't need to engage with that, either. They are on their own path, and it is not up to you to educate or enlighten them. In the process, you could be badly hurt.
– You can also report cyberbullies. Most online platforms, schools, groups, and society in general take this very seriously.

Bullying in all its forms is recognized for the insidious and loathsome social problem it is. Selfish, narcissistic, or harmful behavior is not welcomed anywhere. A growing awareness around these issues means that bad behavior is decreasingly tolerated and often dealt with quickly and effectively. There's no reason to tolerate a bully and no good reason to be a bully. Some bullies may get a kick out of their behavior as a kind of power trip, or by getting their own way for a time, but in the end, they're lonely, isolated, and avoided.

6

Some Essential Life Skills for Kids

It's not enough to just teach your kids good manners and etiquette. Part of the foundation that helps a person behave well and fit into society rests on some key life skills that we all need but that few of us are actively taught.

These essential skills will reach through every area, level, and stage of your children's lives, helping them to be stronger, happier, more contributing members of society.

We cannot rely on the school system to do this for us; we have to take an active part in ensuring our children are equipped for life. I would rather the basics of this stuff come from me, and whatever else my kids learn on this subject additionally can then just be icing on the cake.

So in addition to all the advice about teaching manners in the previous chapters, there are useful associated lessons in how to encourage some of the additional life skills that kids will need to prepare them for functioning well in the world as adults.

Good Money Habits

When you're stressed out about money, it makes managing other parts of your life and mood even harder. Whether we like it or not, money is integral to our lives, unless we live completely off the grid. We need it as a means to an end. It buys our survival. We also want to at least be comfortable in life so that we can meet our basic needs like food, shelter, clothing, and medical care, as well as our other needs like education, creativity, and self-actualization.

We don't want to make it into an end goal on its own, but we do need to learn some basic skills and teach them, in turn, to our families. Some great ways to teach good money habits from early on include:

- *Teach children the value of things*. Let them take real money (not plastic) to the shop and buy a toy or some food. Let them first earn that money doing chores for extra learning impact.
- *Get them into the habit of saving*. Start with a clear glass jar (not a piggy bank, as we can't see inside) and add a few coins every day. This can be savings towards a treat or activity for the whole family, or their own jar just for them.
- *Let them learn to prioritize needs vs. wants* and to make spending decisions for themselves. For example, if they buy that doll, then they can't also buy that radio. They will need to save up for each thing and decide what's more important each time.
- *Link their pocket money to their chores and behavior*. As they get older, encourage them to try new ways of making money, like taking on neighborhood chores, part-time work, or starting up their own little business. Entrepreneurial skills are vital and should be part of every child's learning experience one way or another. It's

a great idea to help them find a job rather than hand out cash for free.
- *Watch your own spending behavior.* Avoid impulse buys and show them how you make spending decisions and savings goals and why.
- *Take them to work with you so they can see how you earn a living.*
- *Teach them gratitude and contentment* with what they already have rather than instilling an endless search for meaning through having more things.
- *Teach them about quality.* Quality lasts longer and is worth investing a bit more in to save overall later. Steer away from brand-driven mentalities. If you do buy specific brands, make sure your kids understand that your choice is based on quality, not status.
- *When they're old enough, open their own bank account* and let them have internet access and their own bank card, too. Encourage them to start saving for college or for bigger things they may want, like a car or a trip.
- *Don't just hand everything to them on a plate.* For example, if they want to go to college after school, how will this be funded? Discuss these issues together and let them weigh in. Look at creative ways for them to take ownership and responsibility. You could draw up a contract where you advance the money and they pay you back, which is probably better than piling up interest on a student loan as well.
- *Teach them about credit and how much it costs them.* Some people use short-term credit well, while others get locked into an endless debt trap. Show them how credit interest accumulates and use this good opportunity to explain savings and compound interest, too.
- *Start them drawing up their own simple budgets.* There are plenty of apps to help with budgeting.

- *Let them donate some time or money, or both, to worthy causes,* so that they learn to give as well as receive.

A healthy money mindset is priceless. We don't want to live for money or be controlled by it. We also don't want to view it too negatively, as that comes with its own problems and hardships. If we believe life is hard and making money is hard, then it will be. Money is often linked to self-worth, which is an idea we need to throw away in its entirety. We need to view it as the energy it is; something we get for our time and efforts, which we can exchange for other things we need or want. Look at money as a tool and also as a thing that can be managed.

Good money skills can be learned over time, if we're prepared to engage with our current thinking and get clear on what we need to do more of and less of going forward. Even if we haven't had much success in this area up until now, it all starts with one positive step. You can even teach yourself at the same time you teach your kids; that would be a great lesson in turning bad money habits around.

If we can apply this in our own lives, we will go far in demonstrating it for our kids. When engaging with the issue of money, we may find we need to brush up on our skills or practices, too, and that's never a bad thing.

Understanding Time

We want our kids to do well at school and in life, and part of that is understanding how to prioritize and manage their time. Time is all we have; when it runs out, it's too late, whether that applies to a school project, a relationship, a career, or a lifetime. If we know what time means and how to use it well, we can set ourselves up to make the most of it.

When kids are young, time seems endless. Their caregivers and teachers tend to help them manage their time, and, as a result, they're unlikely to truly comprehend what it is. They feel immortal. As humans, we don't realize the value of our time until much later in life.

As adults, we also need to take a minute to understand how to think about time, and some of us never figure this out. We let our minds time travel into the past where we dwell on memories that have no lessons left to share, and we often feel guilt or sadness as a result. We let our minds hurtle into the future where we picture endless possibilities or fearful unknowns and let anxiety and worry take us over.

So, when teaching children about time, we want to let them internalize an idea of it, but we also want them to be the master of it and not the other way around.

- **Teach your children how to focus on the present moment**. The ability to focus is learned, by the way. It doesn't come naturally to anyone, so we need to practice it in order to get better at it. Kids have limited attention spans, and this skill of focus will demand a lot of extra help from our side. Even adults are very good at being distracted; by our devices, our busy lives, and all the rest. If we can't learn to focus our attention on what we choose, we'll battle to get anything done. Yes, it can be useful to look at the past to take various lessons from it, but then we need to bring our attention back to now. Yes, we should be making some plans for the future, but then we need to bring our attention back to this moment. It's in this moment that we find inner peace, energy, mastery of our lives, and a meaningful life experience. It's now that we need to give most of our attention to so that we can be effective, complete what is before us to do, and also fully enjoy our life experience. By simply asking yourself "Am I in this moment?" you bring your focus back into the present. Mind exercises like mindfulness and meditation also help strengthen our focus muscles.

- **Part of focusing is learning to stay with a task until it's completed**, or until the part we decided we need to do for now is done. Don't forget the attention spans we mentioned earlier when deciding how long your child is able to stay busy with a task. Around 20 to 30 minutes is the most I expect a teen (or adult, for that matter) to focus intently on one thing, especially if it's an intense learning task.
- **Help them break tasks down into smaller steps** that fit within their attention span. Encourage mini breaks in between bursts of attention. Show them how to get up, stretch, do a small chore or activity, and then return to the main task after the set break time.
- **Discourage multi-tasking**. All the evidence is in that our brains can only really do one conscious job at a time. Each time we switch between different tasks or activities, our brain loses time while it adjusts to the new requirements. So multitasking is not as effective as some people like to think it is.
- **Teach prioritization**. What is urgent and needs to happen right away and what isn't and can happen later? What's important and has to be put into our plans, and what's not important that we can let someone else do, put off until later, or even choose not to do?
- **Start children young** with events linked to routines, like after or before a certain meal or activity. Little children can't understand time so well, but they will most likely understand that you will pick them up them from playschool after their nap.
- **When they're old enough—around six or so—they can start learning how to tell time on a digital and**

traditional clock face. They can start linking how long it takes to do certain things with their set routines and schedules. For example, school takes five hours, then we have lunch for half an hour, then we do our homework for one hour, and you can play until dinner at 6 p.m. Dinner takes one hour, and then we do our chores for half an hour, and so on.
- **Get a family calendar and let them help you populate it**. While doing so, you can talk about developing the good habit of writing things down so we don't forget, prioritizing, and planning.
- **Buy them their own diary** to write down activities and events, plus any projects or goals. Check it together with them regularly to make sure they aren't overscheduling or overestimating how much time they have for these things.
- **Help them set goals and break them down into smaller steps**, then attach a time value to each step. See if they can meet or beat the time you both agreed each step needed.
- **Teach them to build some time into their daily lives for self-care and free time**.
- We know that there are often unexpected events that can eat into our time, or that it might take us longer to complete a task for some reason. So, we can **share how to build a little bit of extra time into the schedule to account for the unexpected**. If it's not used, it can be free playtime.
- **Be sure to reward your kids** when they show good time management skills.

A stitch in time saves nine, or so the old saying goes. If your family learns to use these simple time management skills, it will give them an advantage to succeed in whatever they take on. All of these suggestions help with the steady progress we need to make every day to achieve our greater goals.

Finding Your Way Around

Anybody who has had a toddler or young child go awol when out in public knows the stress involved. It's even more scary and frustrating for the child who doesn't know where they are or how to find their way back to you.

Try these ideas for fewer navigational problems for all:

- Use a toddler safety device, like a cord with a wrist attachment for both of you or a toddler safety harness so they have freedom to walk, just not too far.
- You can get luggage tags with a GPS locator that links to your phone. Slip one onto a wristband or your toddler's clothes to keep track.
- As soon as they are big enough to understand, create some ground rules. For example:

  – If you can't see me, I can't see you, so always make sure you can see Mommy or Daddy. Don't go where you can't see us because then we can't look after you and protect you.
  – If you get lost, go to an adult like a shop assistant or policeman and ask for help.
  – Teach them to recite their name, your name, and your phone number and address. Make it into a rhyme or a song so they can more easily remember it.

- Make a place a central return point in case anyone gets lost. With my kids, I would choose the information kiosk or a specific landmark or shop entrance, and if anyone did stray, they would know to go straight there

and wait until I came to get them. The key is that the child knows they must wait there and not go wandering all around.
- When your kids are a bit older (around six and above), you can start teaching them how to use the map apps on their devices, and also how to read an actual map. Following a map is a really useful skill, particularly when all your devices are dead or out of range.

– Start with small maps, like the garden or park. Show them what north is and how to orient a map based on landmarks.
– You can do little treasure hunts with maps to encourage map-reading and make it fun. Older kids love geocaching, which is an international activity you can try out. People hide small items at a geocached location, and your kids have to use coordinates to find the spot. You can then take an item and leave another behind for the next geocaching team to find.
– Get them outdoors into a national park or wilderness trail and let them find their way with the map these places generally provide.

It might seem like a waste of time to teach map-reading and navigational skills to our kids when we normally have location apps just a click away, but both sets of skills—the manual and the digital—are useful. This type of skill gives kids a lot of self-confidence and added security. It helps them develop critical thinking and problem solving. After all, if you can find your way on a map, it means you'll always know where you are.

These are not the only life skills your children will need, but they're a great start. They will certainly help your children do better on their life journey.

7

Teaching Kids Self-Care

Looking after yourself is a much-overlooked essential set of skills that is less about concrete issues like time and money and more about resilience and a happier, more contented life. Self-care is not just about giving yourself treats and taking long bubble baths. It means getting your physical, mental, and emotional basics right so that you can go the distance.

Having these soft skills will enable your child to bounce back from challenges and hardship, and to have the strength to face whatever life throws their way. Quite frankly, if you don't manage yourself and your self-care properly, having any sort of manners becomes more or less impossible. A hungry, tired, sick, anxious, or depressed person is vulnerable and hasn't got the energy or motivation to deal with very much else. If our basics aren't in place, we're less tolerant, less well-behaved, and life is more difficult all around.

When faced with an unhappy and badly behaved child, some of my first questions are always to do with the stuff in this chapter. There is no way I can expect a child (or anyone, for that matter) to behave, learn, or succeed if these essentials are not in place.

What Your Body Needs

Strong bodies mean strong minds and hearts. What do we have to put in place and be mindful of for this to happen?

> • A lot has been said in print and the media about healthy diets for kids. A lot of bad behavior is often blamed on too much sugar, food additives, and other dietary matters. Honestly, each child is a complex being, and I would look wider than this when troubleshooting behavioral issues. However, diet can and does play a big part in mood management. Our brain-body link means that if we put junk into our systems, it travels to our brains and inflames and damages brain cells. It messes with our sugar levels, over- or under-energizing our systems. It also inflames our gut, which also plays an important part of our overall health and mood. This is really oversimplifying things, but it comes down to being mindful of what we put into our mouths.
>
> In general, it's best to avoid added sugars, fats, and processed foods with any kind of chemical additives. These all unbalance our bodies. In a nutshell, we are still set up in the same way we were thousands of years ago, and so our bodies don't know what to do with all the modern ingredients; the extra sugar, fat, and chemicals. It creates systemic confusion. Things don't work so well, and then we get ill, tired, and out of sorts.
>
> The healthy route is to go for whole foods cooked from scratch or sourced from suppliers who understand healthy eating. Variety in food type and color helps ensure you are giving your kids a wide range of nutrients. Choose from vegetables, fruits, whole grains (brown rice, pasta, and flour), lean meats, dairy (especially yogurts with live cultures for gut health), nuts, legumes, seeds, and fish, especially fatty fish that are high in omega oils.

Of course, kids love sweet stuff, but you can limit this or replace it with sweet fruits like berries and bananas. A sweet tooth is learned and can be unlearned. When you fill your diet with loads of extra sugar, you get used to the taste and it can become a comfort eating issue, too. Cutting back on sugar brings the flavors of food back to life and helps your body regulate and metabolize natural sugars better. It can also improve lifestyle issues like diabetes and many allergy problems, for example.

Gut health is supported with the probiotics found in yogurt, fermented foods, and supplements. Research increasingly links a healthy stomach to a healthy brain, and therefore better moods.

Hydration is also a big part of a healthy diet. Children between the ages of one and three need around four cups of liquids; up to age eight, about five cups; and older, up to eight cups a day. This can include water, watered-down fruit juices, milk, herbal teas, and so on. Avoid sugary sodas and too much high-sugar fruit juices. If you start this way and avoid too much sugar right from the beginning, your child won't know the difference.

If you suspect that your child may have a food intolerance or allergy, chat to a nutritionist to help you get to the bottom of the problem. These issues can definitely affect your kids' ability to self-regulate.

- Exercise is another vital physical building block. Relatively brisk movement of some sort for around 20 minutes at least three times a week contributes as much to a stable mood as do antidepressants or other medications (Sharma, 2006). Kids sleep better and self-regulate better if they're encouraged to have some form of daily movement. This can be walking, dancing, running, swimming, jumping or whatever they enjoy. Most children don't need a lot of encouragement, but you may need to find out what they enjoy most, as not everyone is big on exercise or sports.

• Sleep quality is also an important good-mood building block. There are hundreds of books written about children and sleep, as this can be a challenge for everyone—especially in the early years. In general, it helps to have a set sleep routine where certain events happen in order, leading up to restful sleep. For example, dinner, quiet play, bath or shower, storytime, and then into bed.

Good sleep means all screen time needs to stop about an hour before bedtime so that the brain can calm down a bit. Screens also stimulate the brain in the same way daylight does, so this reduces natural sleep hormones like melatonin.

The sleep environment needs to be comfortable. In terms of temperature, aim for about 65 degrees Fahrenheit (18-19 degrees celsius), or 68-72 degrees Fahrenheit (20-22 degrees celsius) for infants. Clean, soft bedding and good air flow will also aid a good night's sleep. Sleepwear should ideally be loose and comfortable, and excess light and sound needs to be blocked out. Many parents use blackout curtains and white noise or soundproofing to make sure their kids have an undisturbed night. If your little one is scared of the dark, a soft night light at floor level (so that it's not shining into their eyes) is fine.

• Good hygiene is a habit you will want to start as early as possible. It's part and parcel of reducing the chances of infections. These are all things you can start demonstrating to your children as soon as they start walking and talking. By doing it, they learn it and it becomes an unquestioned part of their daily routine.

• As a guideline:

– Always wash hands before and after meals, before cooking, and after using the bathroom.
– Bathe daily.
– Brush teeth after meals or on rising and before bed.
– Hair should be washed regularly.
– Show them how to keep their nails clean and manicured.
– Educate them on where germs like to breed or collect, like under nails, in hair, and also in noses.
– Basic wound care, including sanitizing and dressing cuts, burns, and abrasions.
– Good hygiene in the bathroom and kitchen and around the house and with pets.
– Good hygiene extends to keeping their rooms clean and tidy, too.

Getting these basics right will help your child be physically well enough to manage their moods and thus regulate their behavior better.

What Your Mind Needs

There's more to life than just physical needs. There is also mental and emotional hygiene, which is an important part of mood management.

Teaching your children to engage with their thoughts and feelings is a great start. If they understand that feelings originate in our thoughts and that they can decide what thoughts they think, they will be a large part of the way towards better self-regulation. Encourage kids to name their feelings and to see them as okay to have but also as messengers or indicators of what might be wrong. If we have met all our body's basic needs and we're still in a bad mood, then we should look at the quality of our thoughts.

Are our thoughts:

1. True?
2. Helpful?

If not, how can we reframe them or rephrase them?

Another part of good mental and emotional hygiene is building a strong sense of self-worth and self-esteem in our children. This comes from knowing what our values are, maintaining our boundaries, and finding value in who we are, as we are. We all come with strengths and weaknesses, good and bad sides. Focus your kids on their strengths and their good sides rather than their weaknesses if you want to see them blossom and grow. Catch them doing stuff well and right, be lavish (but specific and authentic) with your praise, and tell them when you're proud of them.

Another important part of mental health is the support of others and a sense of connection to those around you, as well as to yourself, nature, pets, and even a spiritual source. Isolation is one of the leading reasons for mental dis-ease and problems. When your child is challenged, pull together as a family to help them. Let them know they have backup and people who are looking out for them. This sense of belonging and connection will increase their sense of security and general mental well-being.

Part of mental resilience is simply the act of not giving up. To learn to keep trying and not let mistakes lay you flat is one of the most valuable lessons you can impart. Taking problems, learning from them, and just getting up one more time than you fall down means that eventually you will get where you want to be.

Lastly, when your child is acting up, acting out, or seems somehow overwhelmed, look at what you can do to help simplify their lives. Even if it's just a temporary solution, it will help relieve the pressure long enough for healing and strength to return. It's often the complexity of life that wears us down and builds up inner pressure like a steam cooker. So what can be dropped, deferred, or delegated?

Some simple mood management self-care tips to try out with your kids can include:

- Getting outdoors into nature and sunshine (great for vitamin D levels).
- Getting into water to ground and release excess bad moods.
- Helping them put things in perspective. Right now, they're probably not in actual danger, and therefore, although life may be less than ideal at times, they are still okay.
- Meditation or yoga that you can do together.
- Helping them find their own personal power mantra, or a song or phrase that distracts them and also focuses them on more positive stuff. You can even make a playlist of upbeat music to play when they need to calm down or feel better.

In the end, you're aiming for a happy, meaningful, peaceful, and joyful life for yourself, your family, and for your children one day when they leave the nest. All of my recommendations are not some magic formula for everlasting happiness, but each little bit creates a positive shift and moves toward this goal.

Conclusion

> *"I believe that the kids who are labeled 'good' are children who know how to solve their problems and manage their behavior and social life, and the kids who are labeled 'bad' are kids who don't know how to solve those problems."*
>
> James Lehman

It's our responsibility as parents to teach and guide our kids and to be their calm center and safe space when life is scary or chaotic. To do this, we must hold ourselves to a higher standard of behavior. But what I often see is quite the opposite. I see many parents who expect kids to just know how to behave, who don't lead by example, and often behave worse than their children. Then they get angry and impatient when their children don't behave like perfect little robots. I also encounter many parents who just don't know where to start. Nobody has taught them, and perhaps their own parents were absent, busy, or had gaps in their parenting skills.

Until we can exercise self-control and self-awareness, we cannot expect our children to magically do so all by themselves. So good

Conclusion

parenting starts with us. We need to do the work on ourselves and check in with how we're behaving and our own habits and patterns before we start trying to fix our kids. For a parent of an out-of-control kid, I always start with some work on self first. It's amazing how many people just have never been taught how to manage themselves and their emotions, what to do when they feel angry or overwhelmed, or what is socially acceptable. How, then, can we expect them to teach their own kids? These are not 'bad' parents, just as their kids are not 'bad' kids. Given half a chance and the right direction and guidance, they make the effort to be better and to do better.

There are also loads of busy, overworked, tired parents just trying to do their best. Some days we get it right, and others we know we slipped up, but on average our children get a good grounding and the guidance they need. What's more, we're seeing more learning and behavior-challenged children than ever before. Whether these issues were just undiagnosed before or misunderstood, it's still curious how these numbers have spiraled in the last generation or two. Having a child with these problems is even more demanding on the parents. This is when we need all our self-care, self-awareness, and all the support we can get from our friends, family, and community. And yet, with growing awareness around parenting issues, we find that people are parenting more consciously and positively, perhaps, than ever before. As a result, many kids who stretch us in the early years end up perfectly happy, stable, and productive within the social system later.

So perhaps part of my message is to not give up. Ditch those rotten, unhelpful labels and see your kids for who they are, not who you want them to be. Find their strengths and focus on those. Be patient, persistent, and consistent. If we want our children to grow up resilient, we need to be resilient parents. We have to use every tool at our disposal to help us on our parenting journey.

Conclusion

We all have moments when we wish the ground would swallow us. Those times when our children do and say things that shock, startle, and dismay us. No matter what kind of superstar parents you might be, the odds are that at some point you will need to draw on your reserves of calm and patience.

Having a game plan for these challenging times is essential.

First, we need to understand what our children are capable of and able to do. There's no point expecting grownup behavior from little kids, you're very unlikely to get it. You may as well expect a fish to ride a bicycle, as they say. Of course, each child will have their own unique personality and abilities, and so understanding what to expect at each age and stage is really a guideline. Look at your child. Really look, objectively, and let go of whatever dreams, fantasies, or filters and biases you have. They just muddy the waters and obscure the situation. It's essential to see where you are in order to know where you need to go next. You will have to face the facts to start solving any problems effectively. If you're unsure, ask an expert or your inner circle about what they see, too. Then tailor your responses and expectations to what's in front of you.

As you embark on this path, you will also learn a lot about yourself. My children have been my teachers in so many ways. They've taught me patience and how to play again. They've taught me to slow down and enjoy the simple things in life, and they've made me look time and again at who I am, how I'm acting and what I'm doing. There's nothing like kids for helping you get insight into yourself and motivating you to do better.

Then we need to take a little guided tour around the world of manners and etiquette. Not everyone knows this stuff. Unless someone taught you, how can you know? So going over what is socially acceptable and appropriate can help us refresh our own knowledge so that we can pass that on to our kids, too.

Conclusion

Good manners may seem like some sort of old-world, upper-class pretension, but really they are the grease that helps the wheel of society turn. They help reduce conflict, avoid problems, and aid us in getting along by providing some basic guidelines. Let's face it; with growing numbers of people all living in small areas, these guidelines are crucial to enable us to all live with each other smoothly and more easily. But manners are not just the mechanism that enables large groups of people to live side by side peacefully, they're also a way to show honor and respect to others. They communicate a kindness, empathy, and compassion, when used well, that brightens a person's day and makes life just a little easier. Good manners say "I see you, and you have worth. You are worthy of respect." And even when others are behaving like absolute ogres and may not be that worthy in that moment, our good manners help us behave better, and not respond to bad behavior with more bad behavior, escalating and complicating matters.

> *"The test of good manners is to be able to put up pleasantly with bad ones."*
>
> Wendell Willkie

I don't think good manners, or a lack thereof, is a new problem at all. If we dig back through history, we can even see the ancient Greeks and others complaining about the badly behaved youth of their day. We're not entirely unique, although technology, sheer numbers, and lifestyles these days are nothing like the ancient Greeks could have imagined. We are faced with a new set of challenges and the fallout of new systems that we're only now understanding better from a social and child-rearing perspective.

In any event, many of the same principles of personal stability, growth, and happiness, as well as interpersonal interactions, still apply. No matter how different we are these days, how isolated we have become by our devices, changing social and work structures, and busy lives, a few basics like connection, kindness, compassion, self-awareness, and leading by example still work when applied.

I've given you a set of methods and tools that I hope will give many new parents, and those parents tearing their hair out with rambunctious older kids, some better ideas and new things to try. Because life doesn't need to be so hard, and it is possible for everyone to all just get along. It is possible to raise happy, well-mannered kids in positive, constructive ways that don't require any form of unkindness or harm. And that's what we want, really, because each time we harm our kids physically, mentally, or emotionally, we are creating a further cycle of pain and suffering for future generations. We need to break that cycle and do something different if we're going to make this world a better place.

Armed with good manners, we can do powerful and amazing things. And we can empower our children to be good, kind, and successful people. After all, isn't this the not-so-secret, quiet hope of all parents?

Good luck on your parenting journey. If my words have inspired or helped you, please leave me a review and share them with as many others as you can. In this way, we help each other to create the world we want to live in.

I hope that you have enjoyed reading Manners for Kids. I would be incredibly grateful if you could spend a few minutes more of your time to leave me a review on Amazon. Just scan the QR code below or alternatively, go to **www.magletpublishing.com** and click the link next to the book. Thank you.

If you would like to download a free Manners chart to remind your kids of basic manners, head over to www.magletpublishing.com/mannerschart

Other books in the Things We Need To Do series:

Bibliography

6 Reasons Kids Don't Help Around the House | Psychology Today South Africa. (n.d.). Www.psychologytoday.com. Retrieved December 4, 2021, from https://www.psychologytoday.com/za/blog/peaceful-parents-happy-kids/201810/6-reasons-kids-dont-help-around-the-house

Lehman, J. (2009). *Transform your child : a renowned behavior therapist shares stories you can use to transform your child's behavior.* Legacy.

Sharma, A., Madaan, V., & Petty, F. D. (2006). Exercise for mental health. *Primary Care Companion to the Journal of Clinical Psychiatry, 8*(2), 106. https://www.ncbi.nlm.nih.gov/pmc/articles/PMC1470658/

Shocking Results Found with National Survey on Manners. (2014, June 25). Finesse Worldwide, Inc. https://finesseworldwide.com/national-survey-on-manners/

Why kids today are so rude — and why a little bad behavior might sometimes be a good thing - The Boston Globe. (2019). BostonGlobe.com. https://www.bostonglobe.com/magazine/2019/10/22/parents-give-and-give-and-their-kids-just-get-ruder-and-more-entitled/FyKWSq5b1U4aPJMAR6SyDM/story.html

About the Author

Cora Wilson was born and raised in the suburbs of Kansas City (Missouri, not Kansas!). After earning her degree in education, Cora spent more than thirty years in the education system, moving through the ranks before finishing as a much sought-after principal. Her dedication to improving the education and knowledge of each new generation continues driving her. She had dedicated her life to ensuring our children are armed with the proper tools to not only become successful adults, but good, quality people others look up to.

Being a professional educator, Cora has seen all kinds of families. Many of them, through no fault of their own, struggle with maintaining order and discipline with their children. Cora has taken her immense knowledge base and used it to write her first book: *Manners For Kids*. Recognizing that many children are simply out of control and ready to spiral down dark roads, Cora developed a program to help parents and children understand each other better while teaching children the importance of manners and how they can affect their entire life.

Cora is a dedicated mother and soon to be grandmother with a heart of gold. With her husband, she has carved out a quiet refuge in the country where they raised goats and chickens to pass the time. Always a sucker for a good book, Cora enjoys being outdoors after spending so much time behind a desk. She continues learning and developing new techniques to improve the lives of children and hopes her books will provide the catalyst those families in need have been waiting for to get back on track.

www.ingramcontent.com/pod-product-compliance
Lightning Source LLC
Chambersburg PA
CBHW072100110526
44590CB00018B/3250